Roads to Reality

Edited and compiled by
Joyce Blackburn

Roads to Reality

Deeper Life Experiences From Famous Christian Women

Fleming H. Revell Company
Old Tappan, New Jersey

Library of Congress Cataloging in Publication Data

Main entry under title:

Roads to reality.
1. Women—Religious life—Addresses, essays, lectures. I. Blackburn, Joyce.
BV4527.R58 248'.843 77-16032
ISBN 0-8007-0899-7

Excerpt from *The Woman at the Well* by Dale Evans Rogers. Copyright © 1970 by Fleming H. Revell Company.

Excerpt from *The Burden Is Light!* by Eugenia Price. Copyright © 1955, 1975 by Fleming H. Revell Company.

"Chance" and "Circles" are reprinted from LISTEN TO THE GREEN © 1971 by Luci Shaw, Harold Shaw Publishers, Wheaton, Illinois 60187. Used by permission.

Excerpt from *Deliver Us From Fear* by Eileen Guder. Copyright © 1976. Used by permission of Word Books Publisher, Waco, Texas.

Excerpt from *A New Joy* by Colleen Townsend Evans. Copyright © 1973 by Fleming H. Revell Company.

Excerpt from WITHIN THE CIRCLE by Rosalind Rinker. Copyright © 1973 by Rosalind Rinker. Used by permission.

Excerpt from *Sparrow on the House Top* by Ruth Hunt. Copyright © 1976 by Fleming H. Revell Company.

Excerpt from SAY "YES" TO LIFE! by Anna B. Mow. Copyright © 1961 by Zondervan Publishing House. Used by permission.

Excerpt by Edith Schaeffer is from *What Is a Family?* Copyright © 1975 by Edith Schaeffer. Published by Fleming H. Revell Company. Used by permission.

"I Am a Part of You, Lord," "I Am in a Wilderness Today, God," "You Are the Fountain, Lord," and "Grant Me the Kind of Love" are from *I Need a Miracle Today, Lord* by Wilma Burton. Copyright 1975, Moody Press, Moody Bible Institute of Chicago. Used by permission.

"The Cardinal" is taken from *Living With Depression—and Winning* by Sarah Fraser, copyright 1975 by Tyndale House Publishers, Wheaton, Illinois. Used by permission.

Excerpt from *Mourning Song* by Joyce Landorf. Copyright © 1974 by Fleming H. Revell Company.

"The Heart Held High," "The Other Side," and "Remembered Sin" are from *Her Best for the Master* by Martha Snell Nicholson. Copyright 1964. Moody Press, Moody Bible Institute of Chicago. Used by permission.

"He Giveth More" by Annie Johnson Flint reprinted by permission of Evangelical Publishers, Toronto, Canada.

Excerpt from *The Hiding Place* by Corrie ten Boom with John and Elizabeth Sherrill. Copyright © 1971 by Corrie ten Boom and John and Elizabeth Sherrill. Published by Chosen Books, Inc. Used by permission.

Excerpt from *Adventures in Prayer* by Catherine Marshall. Copyright © 1975 by Catherine Marshall. Published by Chosen Books, Inc. Used by permission.

"No Limits on Love" from HOW CAN I FIND YOU, GOD? by Marjorie Holmes. Copyright © 1975 by Marjorie Holmes Mighell. Reprinted by permission of Doubleday & Company, Inc.

TO Elsie Goodwillie
who is blessedly real

Contents

Renewal

Preface

If your reading time is as limited as mine, this anthology will be useful in enabling you to reap the most benefits of this time. These writings by contemporary women, taken from books which grew out of their firsthand adventuring with God, have been selected in response to many suggestions and requests.

First, these chapters will provide the seasoned reader with a sampling of favorite authors who influence our thinking, confirm our faith, and lead us to transforming discoveries.

Then, there is the new reader who may not be acquainted with the various subjects and styles represented here. Some of the authors are prominent speakers, but their books vastly extend their ministries. This will become evident as you read. I predict that it will seem the authors are "talking" just to you.

The choice of material has been made with a variety of readers in mind. While we are members of a worldwide fellowship, our respective needs are uniquely personal. For example, you may wish for the holy exuberance communicated by a Corrie ten Boom, and I may be freed by the intellectual candor of an Eileen Guder. Therefore, an attempt has been made to match a variety of readers with a stimulating selection of authors.

"To one has been given a trumpet, to another a lamp, to another a spade." One is like an eye—a seer of visions. Another is like a hand—genius of practicality. Still another defies practicality and reason and leaps into the unknown, only to arrive in the arms of nail-scarred Love. Our combined insights are manifold, but He blends them into a harmonious whole.

If you catch yourself thinking: "This is exactly the way I feel"; "this is the way the Lord revealed His unchanging nature to me"; "this is the healing I crave in my sorrow"; "these are the memories I hope my children will keep"; or if you are enriched by having identified with and shared these experiences—whether fear or joy, depression or humor, relationships or renewal, grief or celebration—this book of selected passages will serve a creative purpose.

Experience as a goal in itself often becomes little more than idolatry or an escape into ecstasy, but when shaped and energized by the Lord we follow, experience glows with the stamp of the *real.* After all, experience is what we live. It cannot become static. It is ongoing like a road which leads to an expanding world. It prepares us for the next stretch of travel. It illuminates our progress—no matter how limited—through each day. And at your side and mine is the gracious, attentive Companion who says, "I am the way, the truth, and the life." He alone can say it, for He is Reality.

JOYCE BLACKBURN

Roads to Reality

CONVERSION

Dale Evans Rogers

The Woman at the Well

Dale Evans Rogers and husband, Roy, are among the best-known Christians in the Hollywood community of top entertainers. More important to Dale than professional success is her marriage, family, and the communication of Jesus' love. Her numerous books, revealing intimate grief and triumph, have inspired her fans to claim the joy and spiritual power that Dale radiates.

We were sitting on our horses in the chutes of a rodeo at the Chicago Stadium late that fall of 1947, waiting to be announced, when Roy asked me, "What are you doing New Year's Eve?"

I had no plans for New Year's Eve—which was months away!

"Well, then, why don't we get married?"

And, what do you think I said to that?

You're right. That's exactly what I said.

Two old friends, Bill and Alice Likins, asked us if we wouldn't like to be married in their beautiful home on the Flying L Ranch, near Oklahoma City, and we accepted the invitation almost before it was out of their mouths. This was good; it would save us from the usual spectacle atmosphere that always prevailed when movie stars had a wedding in Los Angeles. We wanted a quiet wedding, with as little publicity as possible. Art Rush (who was still Roy's agent and manager) and his lovely wife would be the only attendants, and Bill Likins would give me away.

We did get one piece of publicity, even though we thought we were keeping it all a secret. On a radio broadcast, Louella Parsons broke the news that we were to be married, and where—and she also told the world that I had a grown son. I was frightened at first, then relieved beyond words that the long deception about Tom was over at last. Tom and Roy liked it, too. These two had come to respect and admire each other deeply. Roy was impressed with the way Tom had conducted himself, with his musical ambition, his practical Christianity and his love of little children.

Thank you, Louella: you solved a real problem for me and I'll never forget it!

New Year's Eve came—with increasingly dismaying gusts of sleet and snow. The wedding was planned for 5 P.M., and by four o'clock most of the guests had made it to the ranch, with congratulations for us and something less than congratulatory remarks about the storms they had struggled through. My mother, my father and my aunts arrived from Texas. Tom and Barbara and Barbara's sister were the last to arrive, after a real ordeal with the snow—*and* a leaky radiator—from Los Angeles.

So the guests were all there, and we could get going. Then we discovered that Bill Alexander, a close friend and pastor of First Christian Church in Oklahoma City, hadn't put in an appearance. No minister, no wedding! Bill was nearly *two hours* late. The storm was bad around Oklahoma City, and he had the worst fight of all of us to get through to the Flying L. We were so glad to see him, when he blew in through the front door, that we didn't notice his old frontier clothes. With frock coat and string tie, he was decked out as he thought a marrying parson on the old frontier should be garbed. We didn't even notice it, until the ceremony was about to begin!

Roy was as nervous as a kitten up a tree. I laughed at him. These men! I laughed too soon.

As I was dressing for the ceremony, a strong chill of foreboding rushed over me. I suppose most brides go through the same experience, but I wasn't thinking of most brides that day—only of me. I'd been married before, and it hadn't worked. Was I sure this time? I was alone in the room, all by myself, with no one to help me, no shoulder to cry on. For the first time in my life, I knew how much I needed *God!* I ran into an empty clothes closet, shut the door and just stood there, my heart pounding like mad. It was as though I were standing on a mountain top, before an awesome, questioning God. I felt weak and inadequate—and I *knew* I couldn't go through with this marriage without His help. Haltingly, I prayed.

"Dear God, You know who I am and what I am and what I have been. You know what a great responsibility I am taking on marrying this man with three motherless children. You know the problems that will come. Please help me. Help me with the courage and the understanding to establish a Christian home for these children—the kind of home You gave me. If You don't, I'll never make it."

I didn't hear any bells, or have any bluelighted vision as I said, "Amen," but a deep, reassuring, strengthening calm welled up in my heart. It was like the floodgates of a dam opening to set free the deep waters in which I had floundered for so long. I stepped back into the room, finished my dressing, and heard the strains of "Here Comes the Bride" from downstairs.

Bill Likins gave me his arm, and we walked into the big den and took our places before the huge fireplace. Bill Alexander was there, all set to start the ritual; Mary Jo Rush, my matron of honor, came up beside me, and we stood silently waiting for Roy and Art Rush, his best man. We waited five long, long minutes—and no Art, no Roy! I almost ran for the nearest exit. Finally they came, almost running into the room, looking a little disheveled and out of breath. I looked daggers at Roy; he just stood there and rolled his eyes toward heaven. I swear, I hardly heard Bill Alexander read the ceremony. When it was over, Roy kissed me and Art Rush exploded, "What a way to start a wedding—with the house on fire!"

It seemed that someone had thrown a smouldering cigarette into a trash basket, igniting the paper in the basket and the curtains hanging above. As Art and Roy passed the door of the room, they saw the flames, dashed in and put them out, and rushed on downstairs for the ceremony.

The storm had become a blizzard as the reception line formed; we had to send for the state troopers to help the guests find the motels in which they were to spend the night. It was wild, but nobody complained—least of all the two principals of the wedding.

It took two days to clear. The second night of our honeymoon, Roy suggested that it was a nice clear night for coon hunting. I looked out of the window at patches of snow still on the ground, and I almost said, "Man, you've got to be kidding"—but I didn't. The minister had said "for better or for worse," and while this was definitely worse, the better was that Roy had just promised to attend church with me the next Sunday, so—I went on the hunt.

Have you ever gone coon hunting? It's something. You tramp around in the cold dark following the hounds; every once in a while they let out a yelp, as though they were hot after the coon—just to keep you interested. You stumble over rocks and stumps and holes in the ground, with only a flashlight to help you—unless you're lucky and the moon is out. It wasn't out that night. Along about midnight the men reckoned that the dogs were lost (I knew we were!) and that we should build a fire and wait for them to show up. We drank gallons of hot coffee and waited, and waited. Finally Roy suggested that he might take me and the other women home, while the other men waited for the dogs. I stumbled through the dark to the car, muttering to myself, "What have I done? I'm no sportswoman. I should have married a college professor." But when we got back safely home, I repented those words—a little. I made up my mind to try to like hunting and the out-of-doors, to please my man.

We went out again another night, and this time the dogs did better; they treed two coons in a big oak, and Roy called me to come and see them shake the coons down. There were seven dogs yelping and jumping at the base of the tree and our flashlights picked up four eyes glittering in the branches. The men shook the tree vigorously, and down came the coons, into the most sickening fight I have ever seen. I let loose a barrage of protest and accusation that made the men stare at me in open-mouthed disbelief. Roy was quiet for a moment, then took my arm and walked me away from the scene. "Maw," he said, "I'm afraid you'll never be a hunter. You'd better not come any more."

That was all right with me. Two coons against seven dogs didn't look like a fair fight to me, and I was fed up and fighting mad about the whole business. Roy explained patiently that the coons were actually faster and more savage than the dogs, and if the dogs didn't get their prey they wouldn't try on the next hunt, and coons were *very* destructive creatures, and . . . . It went in one ear and out the other. I'd had it—for keeps!

Back in California, we looked for a home. Roy's children were still living at Lake Hughes, and Tom was at my little house in North Hollywood, attending classes at USC. We found one up at the top of Vine Street, on the side of a mountain, built there by the late Noah Beery. It was a beauty—a large two-story Spanish home with a glorious winding stairway, the largest master bedroom I have ever seen, and with a wrought-iron balcony overhanging the driveway. The grounds were beautifully terraced and dotted with huge trees. There was a big basement: this would be our den.

We moved in. I'll never forget that day. Furniture and "fixin's" poured in from Roy's house and mine, plus Marion (our housekeeper) and Virginia (our nurse), and a pack of hunting dogs who were parked in a huge pen Roy had started building the day after he bought the place. We opened barrel after barrel, argued where to put the furniture, this silver, this glass, until we could do no more. I cooked a huge pot of spaghetti for supper. What a day! What a home!

But it took more than moving in to make it a home. I knew that, and planned for it. When we had announced our engagement, the studio had said that the public would not be interested in a married couple doing westerns, so I would have to devote my time to running the home while Roy got himself a new leading lady. This was quite an adjustment for me—and for the children, who naturally resented me in the role of mother.

One day while I was arranging the furniture in the living room, little Linda Lou stopped me with this remark: "That isn't your furniture. It's my Mommy's!" I started to rebuke her, held my tongue for a second or two, and then said, as gently as I could, "Honey, your Mommy has gone to heaven, and she doesn't need this furniture any more. So now you and Daddy and I will have to use it." She turned and walked away without a word. I knew this would happen. Roy was working long hours, and I was alone with the children—as *step*mother. I was on the defensive—edgy, and a little frightened. It would have gotten worse if Tom had not walked in one day to suggest that I start taking them to Sunday school and church—that God could help me do what I was unable to do for myself. I thought it over, carefully. The next Sunday I attended the evening service with Tom.

Tom denies it, but I will always believe that he conspired with Dr. Jack MacArthur on the sermon that night. His sermon topic, "The House That Is Built on the Rock," didn't mean very much to me until he began to explain that *any* house built on the rock of faith in Jesus Christ *could and would* survive anything that came up against it—illness, death, poverty, suspicion, greed, selfishness, deceit, lies—you name it! It was as though he had known I was coming to church that night, as though he were throwing his rocks right at me. They hit me square in the middle. I twisted and dodged and squirmed under the barrage, but there was no escaping it; I sat there looking into my heart and hearing it shout, "Guilty, guilty, *guilty!*"

When he finished the sermon and extended an invitation to the congregation to accept Christ as Saviour, the invitation had my name on it, and I knew it. I felt a pull from that altar, but—no, not yet. I still fought it off. Tom read the story in my eyes and he said, "Why don't you go? Why not make it right with the Lord now? Give Him your life, and let Him give you the peace I've watched you struggling for—for so long?"

I was defensive with him: "Tom, I *am* a Christian. I've been a Christian since I was ten years old. Isn't that enough?"

"No," said Tom. "You don't really know Christ. I've watched you reading all those 'Peace of Mind' books, and all that 'Eastern philosophy' stuff, and it hasn't helped you one little bit. If you really knew Him, all you would need would be your Bible and your faith in Him. *You won't find peace until you understand that.*"

I *wanted* to go down the aisle, but I just didn't have the courage. There were voices whispering to me, "All these people will know you're a no-good sinner, if you do that. They'll talk about it, and it will be all over Hollywood in twenty-four hours. . . . Don't rush into this thing; think it over for a week or so." Voices! My mouth opened for me to say to Tom, "Give me until next Sunday; I want to think." (What a stall! I'd been thinking about it for nigh onto twenty years!) Tom's eyes filled with tears and pity. He turned away, without a word.

Roy was away on a trip, so he couldn't help me. I felt miserable and alone, as I drove home, ran upstairs to my bedroom, dropped to my knees beside the bed and cried as I had never cried in all my life. The dam broke, and it all poured out in a long, broken, stammering confession. When I had cried myself out, I started to pray quietly in a spirit of repentance. Never before had I talked with God in such a spirit, but I did now. My whole past stood up before my eyes, revealing all the lost years like an unrolling carpet. I shuddered at what I saw—sin, sin, sin—and all because I had refused to know and follow Christ. I had held Him only like an ace up my sleeve against the possibility of future punishment. I cried out in agony, "God, Lord God, forgive me! Just let me live until next Sunday, and I'll go down that aisle and make it a public confession."

He let me live. When the invitation was given the next Sunday evening, I bounced out of my pew and fairly flew down the aisle, grasped Dr. MacArthur's hand and was ushered into a small prayer room for prayer and consultation with a counsellor. I came clean with God, not audibly shouting my misdeeds but remembering them before Him, asking Him to come into my heart and wash me clean by virtue of the blood He had shed for me on Calvary, to create a new clean heart and a right spirit within me, to break me if He had to but—please!—to take my life and use it for His glory.

An indescribable peace washed over my heart, washed out the dirt there, washed me clean and into a totally new creature. As I got up from my knees, I felt as though a crushing burden had fallen from my back and shoulders, and I felt as free as though I were walking on clouds with my feet not even touching the earth. I looked around me as I walked out of the church. The sky was brighter, the grass was greener, the flowers were bursting with a color I had never seen before. Every tree, every weed along the highway sang and waved to me. How great it was to be alive and free. How great Thou art!

Now I knew the meaning of the words of the Book: "If the Son therefore shall make you free, ye shall be free indeed" (John 8:36).

Eugenia Price

The Burden Is Light

Eugenia Price's "autobiography of a transformed pagan" made her an instant favorite, and her readers now number in the millions. Her twenty-three fiction and nonfiction titles—all in print—have been translated into many foreign languages and are the basis of a collection by Boston University's Mugar Library.

Genie's recent novel *Maria* has the "Oldest House" in St. Augustine, Florida, for its setting. Her own home is up the coast on St. Simons Island.

I had not confessed that Jesus Christ is Lord, but the Holy One of Israel had my attention. My full attention. So much so that, even before Ellen asked me, I said I wanted to go to church with her the next morning which was Sunday.

She said I would have to wear a hat, which I hated to do, but for some reason I had brought one with me and so I said I'd wear it. She was supposed to come to the hotel to get me at about ten o'clock so we would have time to talk a little and get there early. She wanted me to be there before the eleven o'clock service started, she said, because there was one old window she wanted me to see. There were elegant new ones, too, but this old one was the one she wanted me to see.

It was beautiful and misty green and small and up in a high vaulted corner, as I remember it. A big square Cross was tipped sideways in its design of heavy clouds. Light came from the Cross in rays as it burst through the clouds. Rays that had the help of the Sunday morning sun outside.

I looked and looked and looked at that window.

And particularly at the Cross in it. And the heavy clouds.

This was the apparent reason she wanted us to be there early but also she knew *He* could get "at me" there in the silence of the old

Calvary Church sanctuary. Could get "at me" off my own familiar territory.

I was very quiet and kept looking also at Ellen's hands while she sat in silent prayer. I knew they hadn't always looked so peaceful. But they did now. And my heart longed for that peace. My hands were restless without a cigarette.

This was the first church service I had attended in eighteen years. I went to my Grandmother Price's funeral but that was all. Dr. Shoemaker spoke simply and with beautiful diction and deep humility about the Grace of Jesus Christ.

There it was again. The *Grace of Jesus Christ!*

I couldn't tell Dr. Shoemaker to stop talking about Christ as I had told Ellen. And anyway I didn't want him to stop. He said Grace was a gift. That we only had to be empty to receive it. That Jesus had sacrificed Himself on the Cross of Calvary not only to atone for our sins once and for all, but to release Grace that was all sufficient for anything. And that we only had to *receive* the Atonement *and* the Grace. At least this is what I remember of his sermon.

I wanted it to be true but whether I believed it or not I cannot say. All I can say is that when he had finished talking about Christ, Dr. Shoemaker, with a Heavenly Light on his face, prayed in his beautiful diction and when he talked to God in the Name of Jesus Christ I longed to be able to do it too. He was on very close terms with God. So was Ellen. They were at peace. Dr. Shoemaker obviously was an extremely intelligent, highly educated man. And yet he lived his life following the Carpenter of Nazareth. He said he was indwelt with God's Holy Spirit. He said anyone could be who belonged to Christ.

I don't know how much I believed but I know I longed to belong too. And when it was time for Communion I thought:

"Ellen has been so kind and so patient with me, maybe if I go up there and kneel down and take Communion beside her it will make up for all the trouble I've been. And also for that nasty crack I made about the grape juice when we first met in August."

Something was said about baptism, but I wasn't listening and I figured no one would know who I was anyway. So I got up and started to follow Ellen down the gently sloping center aisle toward the altar.

She avoided looking at me.

I felt as though I were going to faint and then I was jerked to a dead stop. No one had touched me. But I couldn't move a step nearer that altar where the Communion Cup and the Wafers waited to be shared by those who followed Christ.

"His Blood which was Shed for thee."

"His Body which was Broken for thee."

I turned and ran from the church and headed for the bar of the Gramercy Park Hotel! It was closed until 1:00 P.M. on Sunday! Ellen had to work at the church until 2:30 P.M. I had time with nothing to do. And so, while I waited for the bar to open, I walked round and round the block past Calvary Church and watched the people come out after the Communion Service. A few noticed a nervous woman in a brown suit and a brown velvet hat standing across the street smoking one cigarette after another. A few noticed but New Yorkers and Chicagoans don't notice anyone for long.

So these were Christians. Did I want to be one? Ellen had said there were varying degrees of Christians. Many didn't go all the way with Christ. Many just came to church because it was the respectable thing to do. I thought that was revolting. If I were a Christian I'd want to be a—disciple.

"I'd want to kiss His Feet with the nail prints in them!"

Did I say that?

Yes, I did. Aloud on the sidewalk across the street from the church where the people were coming out to go home after Communion.

But I went back to my hotel and waited in the attractive lounge for the bar to open. About thirty-five minutes I waited. Hotels like this one were so much more attractive than gloomy places like churches.

"I belong here in this atmosphere. Not over there in that dingy place."

Then I remembered the little window with the Cross high in the vaulted corner of the old sanctuary and I thought about Grace. What a strange word for a minister to use. For the Bible to use for that matter. Grace to me had always meant to be graceful. I began turning the word "graceful" around in my mind as I waited.

"To be graceful means to be filled with grace."

Dr. Shoemaker had said Grace was a gift. Released to us because Christ died for us on the Cross.

Christ.

Three minutes to one and I was waiting to walk in when the waiter who had given me room service opened the doors of the Gramercy Park cocktail lounge.

I sat there in the bar until almost two and then went to my room and ordered a large, expensive meal sent up. I asked the waiter to wait while I poured into a water glass the two double-Scotch Old Fashioneds I had ordered. I wanted him to take the Old Fashioned glasses back with him so Ellen wouldn't see them when she came in after her own noon meal was over.

The water glass which contained the two drinks had been washed in very hot water and stood innocently empty on my room-service table when she knocked at my door a few minutes later. She looked apprehensive and was so sorry she couldn't get there sooner. I knew she would be wondering about me because she had seen me run from the church.

People who drink and people who smoke think those who do neither do not recognize the traces. But they do invariably. And she was very, very, very careful with me. I recognized that careful treatment by then and because I had stopped off downstairs I was prone to express myself freely. And too glibly. And very like a phony. Which in part I still was.

"Your church service was very impressive, darling. Shoemaker could have gone far in the theater. The entire thing was good drama."

She just looked at me.

"In fact, I'm quite excited about this whole Christian business."

"Are you?" She sounded far away. On that opposite shore, the way she had sounded the first day we talked in August.

I beat the top of my cigarette with my forefinger.

"I'm not doing a very good job of this, am I?"

"No." I knew she was "listening" to Him again and I was suddenly afraid again for the first time since I "dropped in" downstairs. I knew she had "dropped in" too. "No, you're not doing a very good job." She seemed quietly pleased that I wasn't.

"Ellen . . . ?"

"What is it?"

"What does God look like to you? What do you think of when you think of God?"

"I've told you. I think of Jesus Christ."

I began to walk up and down and it was very frustrating because my loaded room-service table was in the way. Suddenly I grabbed up the old cocky manner and raised my left eyebrow which I always did when I wanted to appear poised:

"Maybe you're right about Jesus Christ. Maybe He *is* God. Maybe they're one and the same."

"Genie!"

"Maybe that's true. And in church today I realized when I heard your minister speak that Christians don't need to be dull people as I thought. I think Jesus Christ is the most attractive Person I've ever known about. In fact, He's just what we've all been hunting for back in Chicago all these years. I and all my friends back there. We're all bored to death and He's tremendously exciting! *But*—I think *you're* far too radical about it. You say I'll have to give myself up entirely and I think that's emotionalism on your part. Or dramatics."

She stood up and was very tall for a moment.

"I didn't say that. Christ said it. It isn't my idea to give yourself up entirely. It's His."

"Well, then your interpretation is wrong. Extreme. Radical. Jesus Christ is just what we've all been hunting for back in Chicago only it's ridiculous to say a man or a woman can't worship God and still be human. Certainly God can adapt Himself more easily than I can adapt myself!"

"Jesus Christ will *change* you, Genie, if you are willing. It's not a matter of adaptation! Have you missed the point completely?"

"No! On the contrary. And I can't wait to get back to tell my friends what I've discovered about God!"

Ellen walked toward me.

"Are you going back to Chicago and tell those people that twisted, distorted spiel about God adapting Himself to *your* way of life?"

I stepped back from her and stuck my chin out and laughed.

"I most certainly am. I think it's a fascinating idea! Christ should brighten things up for us considerably!"

She looked at me for a moment and then reached for her coat. It was a yellow, tweed topper. Something pushed hard against my heart. I gripped my cigarette so tightly it broke and I had to put it out. Even that was gone for this walled-off moment before my last defense cracked!

She wouldn't dare leave me now!

Ellen had her coat on and was at the door.

She had been so patient and long-suffering she couldn't go. But she was going and I knew that if she left me then I'd be without God forever.

God!

"Oh, God don't let her go!" I didn't say this aloud. It screamed through my tightened heart. She hadn't turned the door-knob yet, and suddenly she walked back toward me across the room.

"It won't work any other way except His Way, Genie. Jesus says He is the Way and the Truth and the Life. He says no man cometh to the Father but by Him. Jesus Christ said that. And He's either telling the Truth or He's the biggest phony who ever walked the face of the earth! He also says if we try to save our lives we'll lose them. But if we lose them for His sake we'll find them. We find life in Christ, Genie!"

". . . whoso findeth me findeth life!"

I remembered that from the end of the only part of Proverbs I knew.

". . . whoso findeth *me* findeth life!"

The earth slipped a little beneath me as I stood there clutching the edge of the dresser until my finger with the bitten nail hurt. Ellen didn't smile at all. She was "listening" to Him I knew.

"Genie, you'll make such a terrific Christian!"

I twisted around and fell into the big chair by the window and sobbed: "Oh God, I wish I were dead!"

Ellen didn't come over and put her arm around me the way you would think at a time like that. Instead she said very calmly and with absolute Authority:

"Genie, it would be wonderful if you *would* die!"

"What?"

"It would be the most wonderful thing that ever happened to you if the old Gene Price would die right now—this minute, so the new one can be born."

I stopped sobbing, I think.

We don't remember.

And after a few long seconds, Ellen says I looked up at her. The darkness dropped away and I whispered:

"O.K. I guess you're right."

Then Light.

Ellen has wondered many times since then if what she did was right. Rather what she did not do. We didn't pray. I was so touchy and Ellen had never led anyone to Christ before. And anyway I had been praying out of Isaiah and the Psalms and wordless cryings of my own all week long! This was just the step into freedom and neither of us did anything after it. We just sat there that autumn afternoon in the peace and the quiet of His Presence and let Him be all around us. That I was truly born again from above no one has ever doubted.

Luci Shaw

Listen to the Green

Luci Shaw, wife of publisher Harold Shaw and mother of five, has won critical acclaim from scholars and "just readers" with her books *Listen to the Green* and *The Secret Trees.* Luci's excellent collections have returned verse to the mainstream of evangelical literature, as she dares us to discover fresh truth through her original style, wit, compassion, and spiritual vitality.

Chance

Did God take his chances
on a son sent to fill flesh?
Was metamorphosis
a divine risk?

Once embodied
might he not find
earth's poignancies too sharp,
sweet flesh too sweet
to soon discard?
Might not man's joys
  (the growing
  of body mind and will,
  knowing
  companionship,
  the taste of shared bread,
  the smell of olives
  new-carved wood, and wine,
  morning's chill
  on a bare head,
  rough warm wool,

a near, dust-blue Judean hill,
evening's shine
of oil lamps through an
open door,
day's work, tired muscles,
a bed on the floor)
make up for his limitations?
Might he not even
wish for a peaceful death
from old age?

Ah, Father, but you knew
the incarnation was no gamble!
We are the risk you run.
Our destiny is not so clearly defined.
It's either/or for us.

And when I say you took no chance
on him,
he being our one chance of heaven,
I mean rather
once chosen, he's no chance
but certainty.

LUCI SHAW

GROWTH

Eileen Guder

Deliver Us From Fear

Eileen Guder's gift for helping Christians communicate is extraordinary whether as a speaker, church activist, or author. Among her eight books are *The Naked I* and *To Live in Love.* Eileen's husband, Dr. William Triplett, is on the faculty of the School of Music, University of California, and their mutual enthusiasm for the study and performance of good music has added dimension to her writing.

Nobody Loves a Loser

I would like to be able to say that having found help and strength in time of death that all other problems paled into insignificance. One would think that having found such help that the ordinary rubs, irritations, and common anxieties of life would mean nothing. I discovered to my own dismay that it's not that simple.

After being borne up by what I knew was the grace of God for an otherwise unbearable sorrow, I found I was just as vulnerable to petty worries and annoyances as I had been before. Worse, there was the same old tendency toward self-justification, the same dislike of being wrong, and the same temptation to status seeking. I began to appreciate the truth of Jesus' warning that one day's evil was enough for that day. In the same way, one day's victories are for that day only. There is no carry-over of spiritual success (if one can use that term.) We may have gained in strength, wisdom, patience, or faith, but there is never a time when we can draw upon yesterday's resources.

Fear is still very much with us, a daily adversary to be combated. It takes many forms, but one which few of us escape is the fear of failure. I call it that for want of a better term. When I started thinking about it I realized that this particular bogey is not simply the fear of failing in a particular venture or attempt. It's far more profound than that: it is the fear of *being* a failure. Perhaps a better way to say it would be that it is the fear of being thought negligible—a loser. "He's a loser." How many times have you heard that said with varying degrees of contempt? How many times have you or I said it? In our culture it's nearly the worst thing that can be said of anyone, a greater insult than calling a man a cheat or a swindler.

Not too many Christians would admit it, but we are far too afraid of failure to live in a style that fits our profession of faith. We like to succeed, and no wonder—we live in a success-oriented culture. "The American Dream," a phrase often on the lips of politicians and speakers at graduation ceremonies, conveys the picture of a poor boy rising to great heights. The picture used to include the concept of success by virtue of hard work and honesty coupled with moral purity. It was, we are told, based on the Puritan work ethic; but that particular philosophy has been having a thin time of it lately. The American Dream is no longer a picture of success based on certain highly valued character traits—just success, however we come by it.

Our Cultural Presuppositions

That is the cultural climate in which we live. Success is good, being at the top is the best thing in life. Those who don't make it, who have tried and failed or whose feeble attempts at success never really got off the ground are often referred to as losers. This cultural climate presses in on us from all sides, not only overtly but in countless unspoken messages, attitudes, and assumptions we meet every day. That is why it so insidiously creeps into our thinking as Christians. It can be found masquerading as a very spiritual part of the faith.

We *do* bring into our faith the presuppositions we've grown up with; it would be impossible not to. The old idea that success is the reward of industry and diligence as well as honesty and moral purity has somehow been transmuted into the idea that success itself is the seal of value upon a life. That concept, totally foreign to the Bible, gets into the church because we've brought it with us. It's hard to get rid of.

Making the situation even more problematical is the fact that, for many of us, our first approach to Christianity was in search of help for problems beyond our own strength. We heard the words, "Christ is the answer," and responded to them out of our own helplessness. We assumed that by turning our lives over to Christ we were also handing him everything we had failed to manage, as if he were a divine efficiency expert.

There are those who never get beyond this assumption. They refer every troublesome problem to Jesus' attention and then, having left it to him, go calmly about their business. There will be no more failures in life, because the matter has been turned over to Jesus. And quite often, whatever seemed to be amiss does turn out all right. The point is proven—Jesus is the answer.

But not all our troubles are that simple, not all our sins so easily overcome, not all our situations so easily disposed of. There *are* failures. Some of us struggle for years, for a lifetime, with habits, character weaknesses, or sins that get the best of us time after time. We pray, we agonize, we try again and we are troubled as much by the shame of failing as we are by the problem itself. Failing is so *unspiritual.*

We have fallen into two assumptions because of our American way of looking at life, neither of them biblical. The first, the one we've already mentioned, is that success is the reward of the deserving. We have forgotten that originally the "deserving" were the hard workers, the honest, dogged, persistent fellows who just kept at it. In transferring this doctrine to the Christian faith, the "deserving" have become those whose spirituality merits God's rewards. The second assumption is also purely American—the belief that if it works, it's good. We are pragmatists at heart. And we've done very well with that philosophy, as a nation. We've built a great country, settled a wilderness, developed immense mechanical and technical expertise, and solved a lot of problems. It's been fatally easy to transfer our faith in the American genius for getting the job done into the spiritual realm. It becomes, in its new Christian context, the belief that when things work out right that's a sign of God's approval.

Our Measuring Sticks

There are two ways of judging whether or not any course of action is right. It can meet all the scriptural standards—and that's not as simple as it sounds. After all, nowhere in the Bible is there a handy list of rules for every situation in life. One must be so at home with the Scripture, so familiar with it that the criteria are part of one's thinking, even part of one's instinctive reactions. There is the whole body of Jesus' teaching. There are the Ten Commandments and the whole of the Old Testament law—which Jesus said were fulfilled in his teaching. There are the letters of the New Testament, full of advice and admonitions about working out the timeless truths of the gospel in everyday life. There is nothing automatic or easy about bringing a course of action to the scrutiny of the Bible.

How very tempting, in view of all this, simply to fall back upon all the generally accepted ideas of whether or not a project is right. And so we usually judge a course of action the second way, the same old way we've always judged—Does it work? And by "work," we mean, Are there immediate and discernible rewards? Is it popular? Is it acceptable to a lot of people? Does it make money? We test our Christian endeavors exactly the same way the maker of a new cereal tests his advertising campaign.

Given this blending of faith in Christ as the "answer" (and we seldom define what we mean by that) and of faith in whatever seems to work best to produce the biggest attendance, or bring in the largest offering, or arouse the greatest emotion, we have produced a Christian climate in which fear of failure is as stultifying as it is outside the church. The concomitant assumption is that financial success on the part of an individual is also a sure indication of his spiritual merit.

Thus the church has gradually developed two parallel and intertwined attitudes: that secular success is a sign of great spirituality, and that we can solve any problem by programing and/or organizing. To say that neither of these assumptions is true lays one open to the charge of being in favor of sloppiness, or spiritual anarchy. It is true that the person who is successful often owes his achievements to hard work and discipline and that some organization, structure, and attention to detail are very necessary to any endeavor. But hard work, discipline and the most careful planning and organization are neither spiritual nor unspiritual in themselves. They can be good or bad depending upon the goal to which their use is intended. One can be as diligent in pursuing selfish ends as in serving the Lord.

I am not trying to make a case for getting rid of all church organizations, for abandoning plans and programs in favor of just letting things happen. But I am pointing out that we have incorporated into our thinking, both individually and as groups, an unscriptural assumption that we can judge the rightness and effectiveness of our lives and works by secular standards. We cannot. We have been given quite another way of evaluating what we do and how we live.

The Biblical View

When we examine the Bible carefully to see what God's standards for us are, we find that—unlike ourselves—the Bible is not particularly concerned with success as we think of success. It is not even concerned with whether or not what we do "works." Paul pointed out that the gospel was unacceptable to the Jews, who were looking for miraculous proofs, and to the Greeks who wanted an intellectual panacea. Those who had committed themselves to Christ, he said, were nobodies in the eyes of the world. He went on to remark that God had chosen what the world calls foolish and weak to shame the wise and strong. The "foolish" and the "weak" were the Christians he was writing to and I suspect that they didn't like being called those terms any more than we do. But the point of Paul's argument, found in the first three chapters of his first letter to the church at Corinth, was that our faith is not merely human, but rests upon *super* human resources—the wisdom and strength of God himself.

In submitting ourselves to the guidance of the Bible we are not going contrary to ordinary rules of prudence or wisdom, we are going beyond them. We are enlisted in the service of a Lord who is either ignored or despised by most of the world. In so doing we have already embarked upon a life which would appear to those outside it to be weak and foolish—we are already failures.

Besides that, we have pledged ourselves to the kind of life which pleases God, not man, and pleasing God will certainly mean that many of the methods used in order to achieve success by those around us will not be for us. But when we go through the process I've described—bringing into our faith the ordinary secular ideas of success and workability—we are bringing in an element which is totally contrary to the very basis of our faith. Jesus was not a success by the world's standards.

In order to combat the insidious temptation to evaluate our own lives and our Christian community by secular notions of success, we have to continually remind ourselves of the fact that Christianity itself is in opposition to the world.

I believe that the first question we must ask about any attitude, plan, project, or proposal is, "Does this square with what I know of God's will as I read it in the Scripture?" We must ask that even before we pray. It is obvious that however hard we pray, God is never going to lead us in any way that is contrary to what he has already clearly revealed. If it can't meet that first test, there's no use even praying. The question is answered negatively and the proposal is out.

Once we feel assured of going ahead, however, there is a further test. Every part of the implementation of whatever we do meet the same requirements. We do *not* believe that the end justifies the means, but that the means must be consistent with the end.

Freedom from Fear of Failure

When we use these tests in our individual lives we discover that we are free to move ahead with assurance. There is marvelous liberty in doing something because it is right. For one thing, we usually find that what is right is also what we like doing. It's amazing how many people embark on a course of action not because they enjoy it or because it is right, but because it is socially acceptable or because it will bring money or prestige or both. Those are the wrong reasons for doing anything, and they breed an unholy fear of failure. In fact, they not only breed fear of failure but they are the product of that very same fear. To get rid of any of those reasons for doing a thing is to be freed of an incubus.

When one is doing something because he likes doing it and because it's right he is not only less likely to dissipate his energies worrying about whether or not he will fail, but he is far more likely to do whatever he is doing well. He may never achieve success in the usually accepted idea of the term, which means making a great deal of money or becoming very well known; but he will be a success in the only true sense of the word—doing a job well.

Any Christian who takes his commitment to Christ seriously must come to grips with the question, "Do I want success in the eyes of the world, which may mean using methods not compatible with my Christian faith, or do I want to be absolutely true to God in every area of my life even if it means sacrificing advancement or money?" We must be mature enough in our faith, and in our thinking, to accept the fact that God's standards of honesty and integrity are not those of the secular world in which we live; and that we must make a choice.

Jesus was very blunt about presenting the alternatives to his listeners. He called them to an allegiance to God but always with a warning that it would mean giving up their allegiance to any other gods they had. There was a price to pay for following him.

The price, which is still required of his followers, is that in accepting God's standards of success we may be, and often are, obliged to forego the rewards which come to those who let no scruples stand in their way. To be acceptable to God can mean being a failure in the eyes of the world.

The Church—Another Pressure Group?

It is at this point that we find we are dealing not only with the fears and hopes of individuals, but with the way we are as a Christian community. Although we come to Christ alone and make our decision to be his or to go it on our own, we do not live the Christian life alone. We come into a community of believers. Each one's personal relationship with Christ, important as it is, is incomplete without his relationships within the Christian community. We need each other.

We need each other's help, strength, and affirmation because we probably will not get it outside the church. One of my friends resigned from a coveted position because he could not go along with the shabby morality and unethical practices of his firm; nearly everyone who knew of it thought he was an idiot. "Why did he have to give up a good thing for some dumb academic issue?" asked one man. "You can be as honest as possible, but his ideas are out of the ark!" The words may have been different but the sentiments of most of his colleagues were the same—a man is a fool to allow scruples to stand in the way of advancement.

That is not to be wondered at, it's the way the world is. We all know it. Only in the Christian community, the family of God's people, can things be different. There we can find acceptance based not on what we have achieved in the way of position, power, or money but on what we are.

But can we? An honest look at ourselves as Christians, at our churches and various groups and subdivisions, brings us to the realization that all too often the church of Christ has adopted the same ideas of success that are part of the secular world. There is often no help in the church for the man or woman looking for acceptance. Often there is little help in dealing with the problems a Christian faces in earning a living because he will be judged no differently than he would be outside the church.

I believe we must come to terms with the fact that the bibilical portrait of a life which endeavors to meet God's demands for goodness is not that of our contemporary world. We must grapple with the hard questions of morality and ethics in the business and professional world as individuals; but we must also face these issues and cope with them *as a church*—as the people of God in the world.

As it is now, with the secular attitude toward success and failure often being taken into our churches and invested with a sort of spiritual varnish, we face the stresses of life in a highly competitive society without much help from the Christian community. In fact, we all too frequently meet with exactly the same pressure, the same reverence for success and consequent contempt for those who don't meet the standard, that we have to face every working day.

Getting Rid of the Success Syndrome

There is no quick and easy cure for this, of course. Recognizing a problem is not the same as dealing with it, though we are tempted to believe so. We need more than small group sessions titled, "What is a failure?" or seminars on the Christian's faith in a secular world. You don't get rid of a bad attitude by making it the subject of a discussion group, though that is very helpful. The only effective way of coping with any problem is by doing whatever is right and necessary according to our understanding of biblical standards *as each situation arises.*

The first step, of course, is to acknowledge the fact that we are prone to fall into unchristian attitudes about success and failure. But after that, talking and discussion are really no help unless they take place in specific situations, about specific issues. Fortunately, many of these issues are being dealt with in a far more realistic and far more Christian manner than most of us have managed, by younger Christians. They already have a healthy disregard for much of the "establishment" thinking so they have an advantage to begin with.

One young friend is working as an apprentice cabinet builder because he likes working with wood and has decided that he'd rather do what he enjoys than try for a more prestigious, but less compatible, kind of work. Another man who came here from Europe as a stone mason gave up his plans to be a history teacher because he realized that he really preferred working with stone and had planned to teach because it seemed more acceptable socially.

We will not all have such clear-cut choices to make, but we'll have choices. It may be nothing more weighty than whether I will prepare a company dinner of beef Wellington because it is impressive and my reputation as a hostess will be enhanced, or a dinner of goulash because it's delicious and will fit my budget better. This may seem ridiculous in the light of all we have said about success and failure, but everything we do, every choice we make, is in some sense conditioned by what we think will make us successful—or stamp us as failures. When we accept the fact that "making it" as far as the rest of the world goes is not necessarily making it with God then we are on the right track.

We may be finally free of the dreadful horror of being thought a loser when we remind ourselves that, apart from Christ, we are all losers in God's eyes. All the promises of victory, all the assurances that we will never be downed, all the stirring commands to buck up and live according to our faith were given to us not as people inherently able to make it alone, but as people who are triumphant because we are *in Christ.* He is the one who is victorious. It isn't true, after all, that nobody loves a loser—God does. His is the only kind of love that can take a loser and make him a winner.

Colleen Townsend Evans

A New Joy

Colleen Townsend Evans, widely known for her devotional books and articles, combines writing with the varied activities of being a famous minister's wife, the mother of four, and a community leader. Having known the glamorous "rewards" of a film career, Colleen's insight into the Christian grace of humility comes straight from a Spirit-filled heart.

The Humble Women

> Happy are the humble-minded, for the kingdom of Heaven is theirs!
>
> Matthew 5:3 PHILLIPS

> Blessed are the poor in spirit: for theirs is the kingdom of heaven.
>
> Matthew 5:3

Poor . . . I can't imagine anyone *wanting* to be poor . . . to be totally destitute, in need, anxious, hopeless, frightened . . . . Surely our loving Lord doesn't want this for us?

And yet, Jesus says that only if we are poor will we be happy . . . . "Blessed are the poor in spirit: for theirs is the kingdom of heaven."

There were many poor people sitting at Jesus' feet when He spoke these words, and He wasn't telling them that they never had it so good. No—Jesus had great compassion for human need, and the sight of the suffering poor grieved Him. Obviously He was talking about something beyond physical need.

All right . . . suppose I were in the crowd that came to hear Him speak—and suppose I were poor . . . . I wouldn't have come to get food—He had none. I wouldn't have come for money—He had none. But perhaps I would have come because I needed something else, something that only Jesus could give me.

Yes—now there seems to be new meaning in the word *poor.* I was thinking of it in terms of the kind of poverty we're trying to eliminate from our world . . . starvation, disease, ignorance. But there is another kind of poverty—one that is much worse and not as visible. There is a poverty of the spirit. And that's what Jesus is talking about in the first Beatitude.

"Blessed are the poor in spirit . . . ." This seems to be the center from which the other Beatitudes radiate. For unless we know how poor we are without Christ, we'll never reach out for Him. If we feel we can take care of ourselves, why ask for help—even from God?

Come to think of it, the happiest people I know are those who have tried and failed—even hit bottom—and then reached out for help. Realizing their spiritual bankruptcy, they asked Jesus to take over their lives. They entered the kingdom through the door of their own need, and they were met by God's grace.

They're not only the happiest but the freest people I've known . . . free to be, to love, and to let God work through them. They enjoy each moment, with no regrets for yesterday and no worries about tomorrow. They don't have to prove anything—they work because they *want* to, not because the world *expects* it of them. To me, these people are very rich—not necessarily in material things, but in the things of the spirit. They possess the peace and joy that come from walking close to God. And yet, this route to the kingdom begins with the painful admission that we are poor and needy.

For me it began during my mid-teens when, without actually seeking it, I had an experience that was both mystical and profound. One evening when I was alone, I went to my room—and found myself in the presence of a blinding white light. It was all around me . . . overwhelming, consuming. I was part of it and it was part of me. At the core of my being—in my spirit—I felt free and peaceful. I was aware of my oneness with all things, all people—and especially with God.

Ever since that moment I have never doubted the reality of God or His presence in our human lives. Although that experience wasn't repeated, I still have the strength and assurance it gave me.

That was the beginning of my conscious spiritual journey.

For many years I didn't mention that evening to anyone except my mother. In fact, even now I wonder about sharing such an intensely personal incident, for I think we are in trouble when we base our faith upon experience or feeling alone. And yet, what we have seen and heard and touched is a valid part of ourselves. For me, that moment was where my pilgrimage began.

In the years that followed I held fast to my faith in God, allowing Him to influence my life but not to guide it . . . I could do that myself. Then, during my college years, I began to feel a gnawing hunger—there *had* to be more to life than what I saw on the surface. We *had* to do more than go through the motions. There *had* to be meaning, warmth, closeness, love. I was hungry for more of God in my life . . . but I didn't know where to find Him.

Up to that point my relationship with established religion had been casual . . . I had wandered in and out of church. Now I looked to the church to show me the way to God. I joined, I worked, I tithed, I tried—and I found only frustration and weariness. The route of "churchianity" was not for me.

By that time I had gone from college to Hollywood where I was put under contract to a motion picture studio and promised a creative career. I thoroughly enjoyed my work . . . it was fun, exciting, and lucrative—and I loved the people! Materially, my background had been very simple, and for the first time in my life I had some of the things I always thought I wanted . . . plus glamorous surroundings, stimulating work, and talented people. Yet underneath the surface of my being—deep down in my spirit—my possessions added up to zero. I had more of everything, but "everything" was not enough. The gnawing hunger was still there.

I felt poor—and in a way that had nothing to do with anything external. My poverty was on the inside. True, I had been aware of my spiritual needs for months, but now the needs were greater. Before, there was always something I could do about them—work harder, try harder, search further. Not anymore . . . I had run out of things to do . . . I had done them all and I was exhausted. And what good were all my efforts? Where did they get me? Spiritually I was bankrupt. Let someone else try.

Someone did. At that most needful time in my life I met a group of young new Christians. They were such warm, real people, and I felt myself being drawn toward their loving concern for me. They became my friends, and I began to hear what they were saying about God.

My friends told me that God was real . . . but I already knew that. They said there is a God-sized vacuum in each of us, and until it is filled with God we will never have true peace . . . I was beginning to know that. But then they told me something I had never known—they told me how to find God!

They said I wouldn't find Him by doing good or by working harder.

They said I wouldn't find Him through any efforts of my own.

They said I would find Him through a Person . . . through a Person so much like myself that He would understand my needs, yet Someone so thoroughly *God* that He could feed my hungry spirit.

At last I understood. At last I had been shown the Way. My friends urged me to follow it . . . to give Jesus my impoverished life and let Him make something useful out of it. And so I did. It was quiet . . . and simple . . . and very, very real. I said yes to Jesus Christ . . . and the God I had known to be real—but far away—came into my life.

What a difference there is between a vague sort of faith and a personal relationship with a living Christ! He has given me direction and a goal—and nothing has ever been quite the same for me. If I had to describe in a few words how my life has been changed by becoming a Christian, I would borrow these words from Jesus: "The man who wants to save his life will lose it; but the man who loses his life for my sake will find it" (Matthew 16:25 PHILLIPS).

Left to ourselves, we find this world a lonely place. No matter how many friends we have, or how big the family, we feel cut off from a warmth and love we can't describe . . . . It's always "out there somewhere"—until we open our hearts and let the Holy Spirit "in here." He is a part of God Himself, and He will keep us company as long as we live on this earth.

In our kingdom-walk we are receivers—doers, too, but receivers first. Yet not all of us accept God's gifts. Some people, because of their pride, cannot reach out and take them. They resent God—and they are never happy.

Pride lives a very narrow life. It must have all the answers and insists on having its own way. It talks too much. It has trouble getting along with people . . . it is prejudiced . . . its ego is so big, you can't help bumping into it. Pride wants too much and offers too little.

Humility is just the opposite . . . its life is full and active. Humility is smart enough to know we can't know everything. It listens, and looks at life through the eyes of others. Humility has many friends because it has time and space in its life for more than itself . . . the door to its heart is never locked. Humility is thankful for all it has, and because it has received so much, it gives unendingly.

Humility opens the way to God and happiness. Pride stands back, hands at its sides, and says, "No, thanks, I can do it myself." Humility is free to admit its need for God and others and comes with hands outstretched.

Thinking about humility reminds me of two wonderful people we met in Edinburgh many years ago. Louie and I had gone to Scotland so that he could complete his graduate studies at New College. We had spent summers in work camps overseas, but this time we were to be away from our country and our family for two years—and we were expecting our first child.

Louie's advisor and New Testament teacher was Professor James Stewart, a man well known as a New Testament scholar and a powerful preacher. We went to hear him preach at St. George's West on our first Sunday in Edinburgh, and after the service we stayed in our seats for a long time, savoring the inspiration his words had given us. He was a man small in stature and gigantic in spirit—a man of natural talents, a disciplined mind, and the power uniquely born of the Holy Spirit in a life. We were so grateful that Louie was to learn from this man for the next two years.

As great as he was in the pulpit, Professor Stewart was even more impressive as a human being . . . and in the gentlest, most humane way. We might have felt homesick those first months had it not been for the many kindnesses he and his lovely wife, Rosamund, sent our way.

They came to see me in the hospital when our son Dan was born six weeks earlier than expected. They invited us to spend Christmas with them and their family, realizing that this was the first time we were away from home for the holidays. And then there were the evenings we and our fellow students spent at their house, drinking Ros's good tea and asking questions of Professor Stewart late into the night . . . . And Ros pedaling over to our flat on her bicycle with flowers picked from her garden, arriving just in time for a "wee visit" while I nursed the "bairn." (We had a baby a year in Scotland, so there was always a bairn.)

The "gift" that meant the most to us came when little Dan was six weeks old. By that time Louie was filling the pulpit in a little country church in Penicuik every Sunday, and we wanted to have our son baptized there. Louie, as Dan's father, couldn't perform the service—and of course you can guess who we *wanted* to do it. But we just didn't have the nerve to ask.

Getting to Penicuik wasn't easy. It meant a forty-five-minute ride through the Pentland hills—in the middle of winter. A car in postwar Britain was a luxury few of us could afford, and so we took a long, bumpy ride on a bus. It was too much to ask . . . warm and generous as Professor Stewart was, he was still a very busy man. A friend of ours offered to do the service and we gratefully accepted.

On the morning of Dan's baptism, I dressed him in his warmest and best, and the four of us took the long bus ride to Penicuik. It was cold and the roads were icy, so the ride was longer than usual. When we arrived at the church I was taken to the vestry. Then, at the appropriate moment in the service, I was led down the aisle, holding Dan in my arms. Out of the corner of my eye I thought I recognized a man sitting in the rear of the church. After the sacrament, I turned to walk back down the aisle and this time I got a better look. I had been right the first time—it *was* Professor Stewart! Hearing one of our friends mention that Dan was going to be baptized, he had come all the way out on the bus by himself to be there. After the service he slipped away as quietly as he came. *But he had been there.* In that act, and in countless others like it, he and Ros taught me more about the Christian life and attitude than all his sermons put together. Truly they are two who walk humbly with their Lord.

To be poor in spirit is to be in touch with our own need. It's uncomfortable . . . that's why our own spiritual need must be filled before we can touch the needs of others. Before we can appreciate the worth of another human being, we must feel that we ourselves are of value. And many of us don't.

It's a funny thing about pride . . . often it's a cover-up for a low opinion of the self. It's a way of saying, "All right, world, I know nobody can love me—so I'll look after myself!" It doesn't even give God a chance.

I have a friend, a very lovely person, who only a few years ago had so little feeling of self-worth that she almost called it quits. She was so desperately in need of self-respect that she was completely unable to give to others. Margot even found it difficult to function as wife and mother, but she covered up her sense of deficiency with a layer of pride. None of us realized how empty she felt inside.

One day Margot felt a mysterious stirring within her. Gently, but persistently, it pushed against her pride until it cracked . . . without quite understanding what she was doing, Margot reached out for help. She began coming to church for counseling, and when her minister realized how deep her feelings of unworthiness were, he persuaded her to see a sensitive, caring psychiatrist.

It's wonderful how God uses time and people. For many long, tiring months the minister and the psychiatrist worked with Margot and through them God was able to bring about a healing in her life.

Margot was driving home from the psychiatrist's office one day after a session that had been a breakthrough . . . a moment when the light of understanding broke through to her darkened spirit. As she drove through the park she began to feel warmed by that inner light and suddenly she found herself saying, "Margot, you're a precious person . . . you're special." Over and over she said it until she began to cry. She pulled over, stopped the car and sat basking in a wonderful new awareness of God's love for her.

When Margot started the car to drive home, she did something significant. She reached down and fastened her seat belt. She had never done that before. She had never cared enough about herself before. Now, in one simple action, she was saying, "God cares for me . . . and *I* care."

Margot was beginning a whole new life that was totally different from anything she had known. Love—God's love—transformed her into a generous and thoughtful person. Being able to receive made her able to give . . . and as she looked around she saw how much she was needed. At last she could look beyond herself to others.

A Christian walks humbly with his Lord, or he doesn't walk the Way. Humility itself can become proud—proud of being loved, proud of serving, proud of achieving. That's when Jesus reminds us of our poverty . . . to keep us humble, He takes us through one of life's many Valleys of Humiliation.

I don't know how to avoid these valleys—there are no detours along the Way. And I don't like what I just wrote—but I believe it.

Many years ago Louie and I wanted to go to Africa. Louie had been there earlier and he had lost his heart to it. I liked what he told me about the country, and especially about the people. In America we have so many external things that our hands do not easily reach out to receive what God offers. But in the Third World, where people have had to struggle and suffer through disease, famine, and poverty, there seems to be a willingness—even an eagerness—to reach out and accept God's grace. The reports we've recently received from friends in these areas thrill us as we hear that Christ is becoming Lord to millions. And even back then, that was where we wanted to work!

Hopefully, we offered ourselves—once in the beginning of our ministry and again several years later. Each time the door closed gently but firmly, and finally we got the message—"Keep serving where you are."

And where were we? Right smack in the middle of affluent America!

Don't get me wrong—it's not that I feel a person has to be economically poor to be humble. Some of the most humble people I know are in our present congregation—and they would be considered affluent. But material wealth *can* blind us to the needs of the deprived . . . exclusive, gracious living *can* make us forget those who know of the gracious life only from movies and TV . . . built-in security *can* make us insensitive to those who have to worry about how they will pay their bills all their lives. Worst of all, more than enough *can* make us forget that we always need Christ.

Gradually we began to understand the meaning in the door that closed . . . we have come to see the areas we serve as bursting with potential for God. We are grateful for the challenge, and truly humbled by it. But make no mistake about it—there are many Valleys of Humiliation in the City of Affluence. We've been through some of them.

I especially remember being installed into the ministry of one of our churches. Our friend, the Reverend James Jones, was giving the charge to Louie when he pointed a finger at us and said, "I have a feeling that in this place you will have to decrease so that Christ can increase."

They were hard words for us to hear, but Jim was right. In fact, he was prophetic. Through the years Christ *has* increased . . . and there *have* been valleys for us, many of them. But there has also been joy, joy in the fulfilling of the promise that "Every valley shall be exalted . . . (Isaiah 40:4). It has often been painful for us to be put in touch with our own spiritual need, but it has brought us—and kept us—close to God. And believe me, that *is* happiness!

Yes, I'm ready now to go on to the other Beatitudes, Jesus. I need Your gifts so very much, and so I'm going with my hands open and outstretched. I want to learn what it means to be a Christian in the deepest sense. I want to become the kind of person You can use.

Happy is the woman who knows that without God she is nothing . . . but that with God working through her, she has the strength and power of His love. This woman will be quick to sense longing in the human spirit, and where there is need she will nourish it. Her humility will come from the very center of her being, and it will never allow her to look down on anyone—not even on people who look down on people . . . . And because her humility is real, she will know a bit of heaven right here on earth.

Rosalind Rinker

Within the Circle

Rosalind Rinker is a born teacher, drawing from her broad experiences as a youthful missionary in China, a campus counselor, and, currently, a much-in-demand speaker. Best known for her books on conversational prayer, she continues to write of her ever-expanding view of God's love.

Security Within the Circle

Unable to return to China for a third term because of political changes, I was thrust into a period of decision which taught me a great deal about finding the will of God. I learned that He guides us not only through Scripture, people, and circumstances, but through our own desires, which He plants in our hearts. All of these factors influenced my entering a small church-affiliated college. Scattered credits from other years were gathered up, and soon I was registered as a third-quarter sophomore, eventually to graduate in the class of 1945.

I enrolled in that particular college because it taught the doctrine with which I was familiar. I was still a product of that teaching and felt comfortable there. I knew the doctrine, had received the experience, and had taught it. We are what our background has made us, so in spite of knowing that I was quietly moving in another direction, I waited. I knew in my heart that I was following the guidance as far as had been given to me, and that ahead of me lay more experiences which would bring the truth into clearer focus.

Every year the college invited a special evangelist for a series of revival meetings. The messages were the familiar homilies, proving from the Bible that holiness of heart and life was scripturally sound and that any sin required repentance.

I don't remember who the speakers were during my years there, but I vividly recall the reactions of the upperclassmen around me. During the altar call when disturbed and guilty students went forward to pray, we were supposed to be praying for them—and we did. But the remarks I heard again and again disturbed me.

"There he goes. I thought he would. He'll find out just like I did—it doesn't work."

"Look at the freshmen going to that altar!" A short laugh of disillusionment. "I did the same thing as a freshman, but no more. Nothing lasts. You're just the same. Maybe worse."

Another would add, "Yup, it's the same old thing. You don't get changed at all."

And still another. "You won't catch me up there again. I've been there often enough. I'll do my praying in my own room."

My private opinion: these kids weren't getting any real help with what was bothering them. How could I help? I knew a way; should I use it? During those "transparency sessions" in China I had learned the power of honesty in confession versus the old rat race of rationalization and generalization. And during that time I also had learned how to face a specific situation and deal with it.

I knew—from personal experience—what was happening down at that altar. It was general, anonymous praying. If you cried enough tears and got shook-up enough, somehow the blessing of God through Christ was supposed to come to you. Hardly anyone ever faced up to anything definite, or at least nobody else knew what it was that shook you up. No objective therapy took place. Consequently, kids were at that altar over and over with the very same problems, and seldom was anything settled. The result was a continual load of guilt which was spiritually crippling. This continues to happen unless the Holy Spirit brings true revival, such as the one among our Chinese students.

So what did I do? I went down to that altar and knelt and prayed with the first one I came to: "What's wrong here?" I asked. "What's the trouble?" But she only cried some more. Finally, I knew what had to be done. I took that student, sat quietly apart from the others, and gave her a chance to unload and face up to her specific problem. Then I was able to help her with definite Scriptures such as I John 1:9.

> If we confess our sins, he is faithful and just, and will forgive our sins and cleanse us from all unrighteousness.
>
> RSV

Word got around that Ros helped people with specific problems. They began to come to my dormitory room, and I loved them and prayed with them. Their needs were like mine because being members of the human race, we do not live without sin and failure. But God does not cast us out; He forgives us, and His forgiveness is real.

Besides encouraging them to name and face things, I added what I was beginning to believe more fully myself: the truth of John 10:28–30—the holding power of Christ's love: and Romans 8:31–39—the unchangeable love of God, the family status, His constant presence with us and within—that nothing ever separates us from Him.

These truths came like cool water to the students: they drank them in, and I watched their lives become stabilized in Christ's holding power.

The Kentucky Visit

While I was still a college student, I was invited to spend a weekend visiting a small mission and Bible school in the Kentucky mountains. The director-founder knew my parents in North Dakota, and he also knew our doctrine because his sister attended our church.

I found myself relaxed and wide-open for more knowledge. I was not on guard as I had been during the first part of that Montana visit with the Lohofs. This friend gave the truth to me in such a simple form that I accepted it at once. I guess God knew I needed it just like that.

He asked me a single loaded question: "For how many of your sins did Christ die?"

"For all of them," I answered.

He held up three fingers and began to count.

"Past?"

"Yes."

"Present?"

"Yes."

"Future?"

"Yes, yes, of course."

I knew the answer then, before he asked the question.

"Does Jesus ever have to come and die again for the sins of the world? Will God ever change His mind about what Jesus accomplished for us on the cross?"

"Obviously not. Of course not."

The truth lay there before me, shining and bright, new and true. More Scripture began to come alive for me relating to the eternal scope of what took place at Calvary.

Romans 4:23–25: the resurrection of Jesus was God's pledge to justify us in His sight, and that was two thousand years before I was born.

Romans 5:6–11: the cross covered my sins—all of them—before I was ever born.

Hebrews 9:23–28: you'll have to read these verses for yourself to get the full impact. Briefly: Old Testament offerings were made continually, but now Christ has come, once for all men and for all time, to remove sin through the sacrifice of Himself. He need never do this again. Next time He comes it will be a glorious appearing, without shame, suffering, or death.

There it was! The reason one can be secure in the family of God—secure in the relationship of being His child: because of the completed "work of redemption" which Jesus finished on the cross and because of His death and resurrection, not because I obey or disobey or keep certain rules. No, not by anything I did to deserve or earn the status of sonship, but because God loved me and gave Himself for me.

All of that makes my being a Christian a real gift, planned before the foundation of the world. The first chapter of Ephesians (see *Living Bible* paraphrase) makes this so clear that I read and reread it in wonder and amazement.

The way I once understood it, you would think that eternal life was dependent totally on what I experienced: For God so loved the world, that He gave His only begotten Son, *that whosoever gets saved or born again* shall not perish, but have everlasting life. Actually, it reads like this:

> that whosoever believeth in him should not perish, but have everlasting life.

What, then, does it mean to "believe in Christ"? As briefly as I can state it, it means a belief/trust of the emotions, the mind, and the will about *Who He is* (His deity) and *what He did* (His Atonement).

I began to realize that all my life I had put the emphasis on *the what* (as it related to me subjectively). Not until I began to accept God's revelation, through study and meditation, regarding the deity of Christ, *who He is,* did the whole subject of redemption begin to fit together and become alive.

The Chicago Visit

At the close of one spring college term, I had to go through Chicago on my way to Seattle where members of my family now lived. I had decided earlier that at the first opportunity I would hear some positive teaching on sanctification from the "other side." Then I heard about Founders' Week at Moody Bible Institute, and the dates were right for me to stop for two days.

I walked into that auditorium, picked up a program, found a seat, and read the day's events. I decided I would take in everything and see for myself what these people were like. Nobody spoke to me, nor did I venture to speak to anyone, but I watched like a hawk. I saw, heard, and felt everything.

I especially remember Dr. Carl Armerding and the gentle Spirit-filled teaching he gave. There was a study on the entire book of Ephesians during the morning hours. In our denomination we had never once studied the whole book of Ephesians at a conference. I soon discovered why: there were too many controversial verses from our point of view.

Were these people spiritual? That was an important test for one from my background. It meant: Were they worldly Christians? Were they separated from the world? I noticed that the women were not as plain and colorless as the women in our churches. They were more attractively dressed, but in good taste. Some even wore red dresses—and jewelry too! (At that time I had never even worn a string of beads.)

They looked nice. Even their faces were beautiful. They looked quiet, happy, and peaceful. I couldn't see anything heretical in their behavior or attitudes either. (What does heresy look like anyway?)

I listened to their prayers and songs, and most of them were just like ours.

What was the difference then?

Through all I heard, the Good News ran like a crimson cord, for I was hearing with new ears. I was hearing that God's love and the family relationship are not earned by obedience, but are gifts of faith. They are forever—now and through eternity. A new security was coming through to me: that of a child born into the family, planned for, loved, and accepted.

But inner freedom to change outward standards came very slowly. Being governed by rules in a book and having them preached to you week after week results in continual immaturity. To become mature a person must develop, by personal experience, his power to discriminate between what is good and bad for him. Teaching discernment is teaching a person to think: not forcing agreement to opinion, but permitting him to learn through the choices (and mistakes) he makes. To experience the freedom Jesus promised to those who follow Him, each Christian must be convinced in his own heart as to the meaning of pleasing God and loving his brother. And this wisdom is a gift from the Holy Spirit within us.

I continued to read Paul's letter to the Ephesians in every translation I could find. It was all there: God's eternal love and plan; Christ, the Cross, the Resurrection. It was finished—forever. I am His and He is mine.

And more and more I began to realize that being a Christian is a love relationship.

John 10: the Shepherd and the sheep.

John 15: the Vine and the branches.

1 Corinthians 12: the Head and the body with all its members.

Ephesians 2:19–22; 1 Peter 2:5: the whole structure of the household of God, each one of us being bricks in the temple of God.

How can mere words ever express the excitement I felt in discovering God's full plan! My place in the family; my place as one of His sheep; my place among the bricks of the temple; my place as a member of His body.

Would He ever cut me off? Disinherit me? Pull out that brick and discard it? Leave the sheep lost and alone? In my right mind I couldn't conceive of Him doing such a thing—nor would I do it to myself. How could He, then, who is greater than I, let anything separate me from Himself? My concept of *His greatness* was growing by leaps and bounds.

I stopped fighting the whole idea and embraced it, unanswered questions included. After all, even the greatest among us do not have all the answers. But, thank God, He gives us enough to bring rest to the inner spirit.

The remainder can wait . . . .

Until the day when God reveals it all to us.

Circles

I sing of circles, rounded things,
apples and wreaths and wedding rings,
and domes and spheres,
and falling tears,
well-rounded meals,
water wheels,
bottoms of bells
or walled-in wells;
rain dropping, golden in the air
or silver on your shining hair;
pebbles in pewter-colored ponds
making circles, rounds on rounds;
the curve of a repeating rhyme;
the circle of the face of time.
Beyond these circles I can see
the circle of eternity.

Does passing of each season fair
make of the four a noble square?
No. For to each the others lend
a cyclic, curving, rhythmic blend.
Remember, spring in summer gone
comes round again. New spring comes on.

The circle in the eagle's eye
mirrors the circle of the sky,
the blue horizon, end to end,
end to end,
over earth's never-ending bend.

The arc of love from God to men
orbiting, goes to him again.
My love, to loving God above,
captures *me* in the round of love.

LUCI SHAW

Corrie ten Boom

The Hiding Place

Corrie ten Boom is known around the world for her indefatigable traveling to proclaim the Good News. Demand for her message increased spectacularly with the publication of *The Hiding Place* and World Wide Pictures' adaptation of the book—the true story of her family's sacrifices to hide Jews from the Nazis, the consequent months Corrie and her sister spent in wartime concentration camps, and her final release. This spellbinding legend of horror and triumph continues drawing empty hearts to Jesus Christ.

From the crest of the hill we saw it, like a vast scar on the green German landscape; a city of low gray barracks surrounded by concrete walls on which guard towers rose at intervals. In the very center, a square smokestack emitted a thin gray vapor into the blue sky.

"Ravensbruck!"

Like a whispered curse the word passed back through the lines. This was the notorious women's extermination camp whose name we had heard even in Haarlem. That squat concrete building, that smoke disappearing in the bright sunlight—no! I would not look at it! As Betsie and I stumbled down the hill, I felt the Bible bumping between my shoulder blades. God's good news. Was it to this world that He had spoken it?

Now we were close enough to see the skull-and-crossbones posted at intervals on the walls to warn of electrified wiring along the top. The massive iron gates swung in; we marched between them. Acres of soot-gray barracks stretched ahead of us. Just inside the wall was a row of waist-high water spigots. We charged them, thrusting hands, arms, legs, even heads, under the streams of water, washing away the stench of the boxcars. A squad of women guards in dark blue uniforms rushed at us, hauling and shouting, swinging their short, hard crops.

At last they drove us back from the faucets and herded us down an avenue between barracks. This camp appeared far grimmer than the one we had left. At least, in marches about Vught, we had caught sight of fields and woods. Here, every vista ended in the same concrete barrier; the camp was set down in a vast man-made valley rising on every side to those towering wire-topped walls.

At last we halted. In front of us a vast canvas tent-roof—no sides—covered an acre or more of straw-strewn ground. Betsie and I found a spot on the edge of this area and sank gratefully down. Instantly we were on our feet again. Lice! The straw was literally alive with them. We stood for a while, clutching blankets and pillow-cases well away from the infested ground. But at last we spread our blankets over the squirming straw and sat on them.

Some of the prisoners had brought scissors from Vught: everywhere beneath the huge tent women were cutting one another's hair. A pair was passed to us. Of course we must do the same, long hair was folly in such a place. But as I cut Betsie's chestnut waves, I cried.

Toward evening there was a commotion at one end of the tent. A line of S.S. guards was moving across it, driving women out from under the canvas. We scrambled to our feet and snatched up our blankets as they bore down upon us. Perhaps a hundred yards beyond the tent the chase stopped. We stood about, uncertain what to do. Whether a new group of prisoners had arrived or what the reason was for driving us from the tent, no one knew. Women began spreading their blankets on the hard cinder ground. Slowly it dawned on Betsie and me that we were to spend the night here where we stood. We laid my blanket on the ground, stretched out side by side and pulled hers over us.

"The night is dark and I am far from home . . ." Betsie's sweet soprano was picked up by voices all around us. "Lead Thou me on . . . ."

We were waked up some time in the middle of the night by a clap of thunder and a deluge of rain. The blankets soaked through and water gathered in puddles beneath us. In the morning the field was a vast sodden swamp: hands, clothes, and faces were black from the cinder mud.

We were still wringing water from our blankets when the command came to line up for coffee. It was not coffee but a thin liquid of approximately the same color and we were grateful to get it as we shuffled double-file past the makeshift field kitchen. There was a slice of black bread for each prisoner too, then nothing more until we were given a ladle of turnip soup and a small boiled potato late in the afternoon.

In between we were kept standing at rigid attention on the soggy parade ground where we had spent the night. We were near one edge of the huge camp here, close enough to the outer wall to see the triple row of electric wires running along the top. Two entire days we spent this way, stretching out again the second night right where we stood. It did not rain again but ground and blankets were still damp. Betsie began to cough. I took Nollie's blue sweater from my pillowcase, wrapped it around her and gave her a few drops of the vitamin oil. But by morning she had agonizing intestinal cramps. Again and again throughout that second day she had to ask the impatient woman monitor at the head of our row for permission to go to the ditch that served as sanitary facility.

It was the third night as we were getting ready to lie down again under the sky when the order came to report to the processing center for new arrivals. A ten-minute march brought us to the building. We inched along a corridor into a huge reception room. And there under the harsh ceiling lights we saw a dismal sight. As each woman reached a desk where some officers sat she had to lay her blanket, pillowcase, and whatever else she carried onto a growing pile of these things. A few desks further along she had to strip off every scrap of clothes, throw them onto a second pile, and walk naked past the scrutiny of a dozen S.S. men into the shower room. Coming out of the shower she wore only a thin prison dress and a pair of shoes. Nothing more.

But Betsie needed that sweater! She needed the vitamins! Most of all, we needed our Bible. How could we live in this place without it? But how could I ever take it past so many watchful eyes without the overalls covering it?

We were almost at the first desk. I fished desperately in my pillowcase, drew out the bottle of vitamins and closed my fist around them. Reluctantly we dropped the other things on the heap that was fast becoming a mountain. "Dear God," I prayed, "You have given us this precious Book, You have kept it hidden through checkpoints and inspections, You have used it for so many—"

I felt Betsie stagger against me and looked at her in alarm. Her face was white, her lips pressed tight together. A guard was passing by; I begged him in German to show us the toilets. Without so much as a glance, he jerked his head in the direction of the shower room.

Timidly Betsie and I stepped out of line and walked to the door of the big, dank-smelling room with its row on row of overhead spigots. It was empty, waiting for the next batch of fifty naked and shivering women to be admitted.

"Please," I said to the S.S. man guarding the door, "where are the toilets?"

He did not look at me either. "Use the drainholes!" he snapped, and as we stepped inside he slammed the door behind us. We stood alone in the room where a few minutes later we would return stripped even of the clothes on our backs. Here were the prison things we were to put on, piled just inside the door. From the front and back of each otherwise ordinary dress a large "X" had been cut out and replaced with cloth of another color.

And then we saw something else, stacked in the far corner, a pile of old wooden benches. They were slimy with mildew, crawling with cockroaches, but to me they seemed the furniture of heaven itself.

"The sweater! Take the sweater off!" I hissed, fumbling with the string at my neck. Betsie handed it to me and in an instant I had wrapped it around the Bible and the vitamin bottle and stuffed the precious bundle behind the benches.

And so it was that when we were herded into that room ten minutes later we were not poor, but rich. Rich in this new evidence of the care of Him who was God even of Ravensbruck.

We stood beneath the spigots as long as the flow of icy water lasted, feeling it soften our lice-eaten skin. Then we clustered dripping wet around the heap of prison dresses, holding them up, passing them about, looking for approximate fits. I found a loose long-sleeved dress for Betsie that would cover the blue sweater when she would have a chance to put it on. I squirmed into another dress for myself, then reached behind the benches and shoved the little bundle quickly inside the neck.

It made a bulge you could have seen across the Grote Markt. I flattened it out as best I could, pushing it down, tugging the sweater around my waist, but there was no real concealing it beneath the thin cotton dress. And all the while I had the incredible feeling that it didn't matter, that this was not my business, but God's. That all I had to do was walk straight ahead.

As we trooped back out through the shower room door, the S.S. men ran their hands over every prisoner, front, back, and sides. The woman ahead of me was searched three times. Behind me, Betsie was searched. No hand touched me.

At the exit door to the building was a second ordeal, a line of women guards examining each prisoner again. I slowed down as I reached them but the *Aufseherin* in charge shoved me roughly by the shoulder. "Move along! You're holding up the line!"

And so Betsie and I arrived at Barracks 8 in the small hours of that morning, bringing not only the Bible, but a new knowledge of the power of Him whose story it was. There were three women already asleep in the bed assigned to us. They made room for us as best they could but the mattress sloped and I kept sliding to the floor. At last all five of us lay sideways across the bed and managed to get shoulders and elbows arranged. The blanket was a poor threadbare affair compared with the ones we had given up, but at least the overcrowding produced its own warmth. Betsie had put on the blue sweater beneath her long-sleeved dress and wedged now between me and the others, her shivering gradually subsided and she was asleep. I lay awake a while longer, watching a searchlight sweep the rear wall in long regular arcs, hearing the distant calls of soldiers patrolling the walls . . . .

Morning roll call at Ravensbruck came half an hour earlier than at Vught. By 4:30 A.M. we had to be standing outside in the black predawn chill, standing at parade attention in blocks of one hundred women, ten wide, ten deep. Sometimes after hours of this we would gain the shelter of the barracks only to hear the whistle.

"Everybody out! Fall in for roll call!"

Barracks 8 was in the quarantine compound. Next to us—perhaps as a deliberate warning to newcomers—were located the punishment barracks. From there, all day long and often into the night, came the sounds of hell itself. They were not the sounds of anger, or of any human emotion, but of a cruelty altogether detached: blows landing in regular rhythm, screams keeping pace. We would stand in our ten-deep ranks with our hands trembling at our sides, longing to jam them against our ears, to make the sounds stop.

The instant of dismissal we would mob the door of Barracks 8, stepping on each other's heels in our eagerness to get inside, to shrink the world back to understandable proportions.

It grew harder and harder. Even within these four walls there was too much misery, too much seemingly pointless suffering. Every day something else failed to make sense, something else grew too heavy. "Will You carry this too, Lord Jesus?"

But as the rest of the world grew stranger, one thing became increasingly clear. And that was the reason the two of us were here. Why others should suffer we were not shown. As for us, from morning until lights-out, whenever we were not in ranks for roll call, our Bible was the center of an ever-widening circle of help and hope. Like waifs clustered around a blazing fire, we gathered about it, holding out our hearts to its warmth and light. The blacker the night around us grew, the brighter and truer and more beautiful burned the word of God. "Who shall separate us from the love of Christ? Shall tribulation, or distress, or persecution, or famine, or nakedness, or peril, or sword? . . . Nay, in all these things we are more than conquerors through him that loved us."

I would look about us as Betsie read, watching the light leap from face to face. More than conquerors. . . . It was not a wish. It was a fact. We knew it, we experienced it minute by minute—poor, hated, hungry. We are more than conquerors. Not "we shall be." We are! Life in Ravensbruck took place on two separate levels, mutually impossible. One, the observable, external life, grew every day more horrible. The other, the life we lived with God, grew daily better, truth upon truth, glory upon glory.

Sometimes I would slip the Bible from its little sack with hands that shook, so mysterious had it become to me. It was new; it had just been written. I marveled sometimes that the ink was dry. I had believed the Bible always, but reading it now had nothing to do with belief. It was simply a description of the way things were—of hell and heaven, of how men act and how God acts. I had read a thousand times the story of Jesus' arrest—how soldiers had slapped Him, laughed at Him, flogged Him. Now such happenings had faces and voices.

Fridays—the recurrent humiliation of medical inspection. The hospital corridor in which we waited was unheated, and a fall chill had settled into the walls. Still we were forbidden even to wrap ourselves in our own arms, but had to maintain our erect, hands-at-sides position as we filed slowly past a phalanx of grinning guards. How there could have been any pleasure in the sight of these stick-thin legs and hunger-gloated stomachs I could not imagine. Surely there is no more wretched sight than the human body unloved and uncared for. Nor could I see the necessity for the complete undressing: when we finally reached the examining room a doctor looked down each throat, another—a dentist presumably—at our teeth, a third in between each finger. And that was all. We trooped again down the long, cold corridor and picked up our X-marked dresses at the door.

But it was one of these mornings while we were waiting, shivering, in the corridor, that yet another page in the Bible leapt into life for me.

He hung naked on the cross.

I had not known—I had not thought . . . . The paintings, the carved crucifixes showed at the least a scrap of cloth. But this, I suddenly knew, was the respect and reverence of the artist. But oh—at the time itself, on that other Friday morning—there had been no reverence. No more than I saw in the faces around us now.

I leaned toward Betsie, ahead of me in line. Her shoulder blades stood out sharp and thin beneath her blue-mottled skin.

"Betsie, they took *His* clothes too."

Ahead of me I heard a little gasp. "Oh, Corrie. And I never thanked Him . . . ."

Every day the sun rose a little later, the bite took longer to leave the air. It will be better, everyone assured everyone else, when we move into permanent barracks. We'll have a blanket apiece. A bed of our own. Each of us painted into the picture her own greatest need.

For me it was a dispensary where Betsie could get medication for her cough. "There'll be a nurse assigned to the barracks." I said it so often that I convinced myself. I was doling out a drop of the Davitamon each morning on her piece of black bread, but how much longer could the small bottle last? "Especially," I would tell her, "if you keep sharing it around every time someone sneezes."

The move to permanent quarters came the second week in October. We were marched, ten abreast, along a wide cinder avenue and then into a narrower street of barracks. Several times the column halted while numbers were read out—names were never used at Ravensbruck. At last Betsie's and mine were called: "Prisoner 66729, Prisoner 66730." We stepped out of line with a dozen or so others and stared at the long gray front of Barracks 28. Half its windows seemed to have been broken and replaced with rags. A door in the center let us into a large room where two hundred or more women bent over knitting needles. On tables between them were piles of woolen socks in army gray.

On either side doors opened into two still larger rooms—by far the largest dormitories we had yet seen. Betsie and I followed a prisoner-guide through the door at the right. Because of the broken windows the vast room was in semi-twilight. Our noses told us, first, that the place was filthy: somewhere plumbing had backed up, the bedding was soiled and rancid. Then as our eyes adjusted to the gloom we saw that there were no individual beds at all, but great square piers stacked three high, and wedged side by side and end to end with only an occasional narrow aisle slicing through.

We followed our guide single file—the aisle was not wide enough for two—fighting back the claustrophobia of these platforms rising everywhere above us. The tremendous room was nearly empty of people; they must have been out on various work crews. At last she pointed to a second tier in the center of a large block. To reach it we had to stand on the bottom level, haul ourselves up, and then crawl across three other straw-covered platforms to reach the one that we would share with—how many? The deck above us was too close to let us sit up. We lay back, struggling against the nausea that swept over us from the reeking straw. We could hear the women who had arrived with us finding their places.

Suddenly I sat up, striking my head on the cross-slats above. Something had pinched my leg.

"Fleas!" I cried. "Betsie, the place is swarming with them!"

We scrambled across the intervening platforms, heads low to avoid another bump, dropped down to the aisle and edged our way to a patch of light.

"Here! And here another one!" I wailed. "Betsie, how can we live in such a place!"

"Show us. Show us how." It was said so matter of factly it took me a second to realize she was praying. More and more the distinction between prayer and the rest of life seemed to be vanishing for Betsie.

"Corrie!" she said excitedly. "He's given us the answer! Before we asked, as He always does! In the Bible this morning. Where was it? Read that part again!"

I glanced down the long dim aisle to make sure no guard was in sight, then drew the Bible from its pouch. "It was in First Thessalonians," I said. We were on our third complete reading of the New Testament since leaving Scheveningen. In the feeble light I turned the pages. "Here it is: 'Comfort the frightened, help the weak, be patient with everyone. See that none of you repays evil for evil, but always seek to do good to one another and to all . . . .' " It seemed written expressly to Ravensbruck.

"Go on," said Betsie. "That wasn't all."

"Oh yes: '. . . to one another and to all. Rejoice always, pray constantly, give thanks in all circumstances; for this is the will of God in Christ Jesus—"

"That's it, Corrie! That's His answer. 'Give thanks in all circumstances!' That's what we can do. We can start right now to thank God for every single thing about this new barracks!"

I stared at her, then around me at the dark, foul-aired room.

"Such as?" I said.

"Such as being assigned here together."

I bit my lip. "Oh yes, Lord Jesus!"

"Such as what you're holding in your hands."

I looked down at the Bible. "Yes! Thank You, dear Lord, that there was no inspection when we entered here! Thank You for all the women, here in this room, who will meet You in these pages."

"Yes," said Betsie. "Thank You for the very crowding here. Since we're packed so close, that many more will hear!" She looked at me expectantly. "Corrie!" she prodded.

"Oh, all right. Thank You for the jammed, crammed, stuffed, packed, suffocating crowds."

"Thank You," Betsie went on serenely, "for the fleas and for—"

The fleas! This was too much. "Betsie, there's no way even God can make me grateful for a flea."

" 'Give thanks in *all* circumstances,' " she quoted. "It doesn't say, 'in pleasant circumstances.' Fleas are part of this place where God has put us."

And so we stood between piers of bunks and gave thanks for fleas. But this time I was sure Betsie was wrong.

Wilma Burton

I Need a Miracle Today, Lord

Wilma Burton, editor of *The Pen Woman* magazine, is a prize-winning poet widely published. She is also recognized for her active participation in writers' conferences and workshops. Her work illustrates that "there is therapy in prayer and poetry, and a double portion of comfort results when the two combine to express the Christian's continued dependence on God."

I Am a Part of You, Lord

no fragment floating in space
but firmly attached
to Your Lifeline:
    "Accepted in the Beloved."
    I am subscriber to Your Salvation Plan:
    this blood that rivers
    in a thousand veins
    You set in motion
    moving ever onward
toward Your Mighty Ocean.
This house, my dwelling,
often needs repair
  and You, O Carpenter of Nazareth,
  are always available
  with Your tools
  for floor, siding, or roof repair.
House of spirit, or flesh,
this is Your hostel, too, Lord—
dwell, Lord, in me.

WILMA BURTON

You Are the Fountain, Lord

without You, I would be winter-grass
brown and lifeless.
    You keep me green
    as watercress in a flowing spring
    in late winter.
There is no yellow leafing
beneath the freshness of Your water.
    Every day is April,
    no summer draught,
    nights are wet dawns with dews,
    mornings are newborn.
Thank You for the coolness
of Your water from deep wells
giving abundance
to what would be paucity,
famine without You.

WILMA BURTON

FAMILY

Ruth Hunt

Sparrow on the House Top

Ruth Hunt, experienced teacher, world traveler, author, has an absorbing easy-to-read way of adapting the solutions to the problems found in the lives of familiar bibilical characters to those of contemporary women—widows, singles, divorcées—trapped in loneliness. With her husband, Dave, and their four children, Ruth lives in Northridge, California, near the elementary school of which she is the principal.

"Call Me Mara"

At the crossroads the three women were having a good cry. They had reason to cry, no doubt about that. There wasn't much more these three could lose and still come out of it in one piece. The older one especially. A widow at an age when she'd have no chance of remarrying, Naomi had also lost the two sons who could have supported her in her old age. And that wasn't all! She was on her way back to Bethlehem after a ten-year parenthesis in the land of Moab, where her family had gone years before to escape a Judean famine. That was where one disaster after another had shattered her life. Now it was empty-handed back to the old hometown to explain it all to the folks there. That wasn't going to be easy either. Bitterly she wept—long and loud.

Today, some three thousand years later, she would have plenty of company, with more than one out of three once-married women widowed or divorced, and an increasing percentage either choosing or being compelled by circumstances to make a go of it on their own. Despite the long way baby is supposed to have come since the days of her chores-children-church-enclosed world, most women still relate their happiness quotient to whether or not there's a man in their lives. We try in a hundred ways to conceal the emptiness, but there it is—that feeling of dependence on an arm stronger than ours and the need for an intimate sharing that seems possible only to those who have been made one flesh.

It's the emotional dependence that's lingered long after Eve was presented as a gift to Adam. A woman wants to feel cherished. There's no substitute for that delicious sense of being desirable, intriguing, indispensable. Neither can anything replace a love that's kind and patient and suffers long, a love that covers a multitude of sins. Naomi must have had this kind of relationship to miss Elimelech so much. A husband—or the lack of one—was uppermost in her thinking, always. A prominent psychologist has declared that half of his women patients come to him because they're married and the other half because they're not. For Naomi marriage was obviously the focal point of her existence.

Of course, like most of us, Naomi probably had her off days when she secretly wished that her Elimelech would just go away on a business trip for a few days . . . a fishing jaunt . . . anything, so she could be alone for a change. The time did come for her—with a vengeance—and she learned what it was to step across the threshold of an empty house. She knew the cold comfort of an empty bed and the silence of a table set for one. The knowledge that the doorbell won't ring at six, nor will anyone answer to one's own knock or call makes terribly real the truth of what God did when He made two *one* flesh. The separation truly is a cutting asunder and it hurts. The future—uncertain and frightening as old age approaches—must now be faced alone.

Whatever the emotional vacuum left by Naomi's loss, the material one was bad enough. No Social Security checks to count on, no tax breaks, widow's pension, mortgage insurance, half-fares, or food stamps. There was no way of earning a living. All Naomi could hope for was charity. She'd lost a lot and she knew it.

Yes, Naomi cried at the crossroads. Thousands of women are crying at that same crossroads today, and crying so loudly that they overlook some of the beautiful solutions that God has placed at their very elbows. For Naomi that key was her daughter-in-law and the way she worked out her own loss. We often forget that these two women were both widows, but so differently did they handle their grief that the one stands out as the very epitome of hopeless sorrow and the other as a ray of comforting sunshine in her mother-in-law's embittered heart.

Certainly Elimelech hadn't brought his family to Moab with any thought of either of his boys marrying one of the despised Moabite girls. Before ever the Israelites had entered the land of Canaan, these seductive women had caused many of their young soldiers to sin and even to sacrifice to strange gods. What an embarrassment his sons' marriages must have been to good, upright Elimelech and his faithful wife, though we know they must have tried to make the best of it. Ruth's and Orpah's loyalty bear that out.

Added to that disappointment there must have been the nagging realization that they weren't experiencing God's best in their lives, either as a family or as a nation. What could you expect, with men like Samson judging the land? The spiritual emptiness gnawed at the moral fiber of the nation just as surely as hunger gnawed at the stomach. The children of Israel were designed with a built-in God-shaped vacuum and only rarely was it being filled in those days. Little wonder there was a famine.

The separations we experience aren't always God's best either. We know that. The death of a beloved husband or divorce from an incompatible one inflicts wounds that our loving Father finds no delight in, but which He can use to make the fabric of our lives work together for good. How do we accept those wounds? With no real hope for a better life, Ruth went, nevertheless, with serenity and with determination. What a beautiful combination—the sweet and loving disposition and at the same time this gut-level moral and physical energy. "Where *you* go, I will go. Don't try to change my mind on that. Your God will be *my* God. My decision's made. Your people *will* be my people. I'll win them over, somehow. I know I will, with God's help."

With all the good resolves made and voiced and sealed with action, Ruth faced the future. And there's the key—that expectation that the future will not be as the past has been. "Hope is . . . perhaps, the chief happiness which this world affords," said Samuel Johnson. "Everything that is done in the world is done by hope," echoed Martin Luther King in a later age. For the Christian there's the added dimension of a hope that "maketh not ashamed"—or never disappoints (Romans 5:5). To the assurance of God's love and faithfulness Ruth added the willing heart that lends hands and feet to His promises.

"You can't go home again," Thomas Wolfe tells us. The joys of the past can never be re-created. We idealize that perfect vacation in

Hawaii and scrimp and save and, delirium of joy, ten years later we go again—and are terribly disappointed. How Hawaii has changed! No. We've changed. A happy experience is unique and it's creative. Part of ourselves is absorbed into that moment or day or special year, never to be recycled. But the beauty of it is that *new* joys and experiences are forever germinating, ready to nudge their way into existence. All they need is to be nurtured and cultivated and coaxed into the sunlight.

But Naomi lingered over the past bitterness as she placed one weary foot after the other. And how contagious her recital at the crossroads was. "God is against me. Turn back."

(*But Naomi, God is faithful after all. Don't you see your daughter-in-law by your side? Open your eyes. Don't be blind like Elisha's servant. There are invisible chariots of fire surrounding you now, holding back the oppressive power of Satan.*)

"See, Orpah has left. Run along after your sister-in-law, Ruth. I'll be (*sob*) all right."

No way was Ruth going to run along, but so wrapped up was Naomi in the total hopelessness of her situation that she gave up arguing at last. What a stubborn girl this Ruth was. Silently the two turned their faces toward Bethlehem and trudged on.

As with so many who face deep and sustained sorrow, Naomi's feeling of self-esteem had suffered. She couldn't imagine that either of her two daughters-in-law really *wanted* to remain with her, even though it must have been her godly life that had won them from their own heathen worship, and there must have been endearing qualities that had won this loyalty to her personally. Ruth had dealt kindly with her and her dead sons. She witnessed to that. But to leave home and loved ones and country to accompany their destitute mother-in-law to a strange land? It hardly seemed possible that Ruth would sacrifice so much for so little.

What a sensation their arrival in Bethlehem caused.

"That woman over there . . . can it be . . . Naomi? What a change!"

"It's obvious . . . some tragedy—but look, the young woman with her. I've never seen *her* before."

"You don't suppose she's one of those *Moabite* girls . . . you know . . . married her son?"

The momentary disapproval disintegrated in hugs and tears as the old friends fell on each other's necks.

"Don't call me Naomi, girls. Call me Mara. The Lord has really been hard on me." *And will no doubt continue to be,* her tone must have implied.

How often when sorrow comes into our lives, our hearts, if not our lips, accuse God as Naomi did. "The Almighty hath afflicted me." After all, He could have prevented it if He'd *wanted* to. He didn't want to, so there must be some defect in His love. It was hardly the way Joseph interpreted his misfortunes. Thrown into a pit, sold to slave traders, falsely accused, cast into prison and elevated at last to the second place in the Pharaoh's kingdom, he disarmed the brothers who'd started it all with the gracious words, "You meant it for evil, but the Lord meant it for good." Joseph's cross was cruelty and injustice. Ruth's and Naomi's was the loss of home and husband and children. In both cases the Master Designer was weaving a beautiful pattern which, from the perspective of either prison or graveside, was totally unrecognizable. Like Joseph, Ruth faced the dark places with serenity and determination.

The babble of voices rose and fell in the dusty streets of Bethlehem, and all the while Ruth waited in her mother-in-law's shadow, eyes downcast, feeling the appraising glances, sensing the veiled implication that all the bad things that had happened to Naomi in her homeland had somehow left their stigma on *her.* Unflinchingly she stood there and reminded herself of her resolve: These people *would* become her people.

What a treasure Naomi had brought with her in this simple, unprepossessing Moabite girl. She was apparently totally overlooked in all of Naomi's thinking. There was love, yes, and gratitude. There must have been some sort of introduction to the townsfolk who gathered that day. "Oh, by the way, this is Ruth, my beloved Chilion's widow. She's been good to me. Receive her for my sake." But Ruth in no way figured in her thoughts of the future. In Naomi's thinking, she'd come home alone, yet all the while the key to a new life had plodded faithfully at her side. She'd come home *empty,* as she had said, but it was at the time of barley harvest. She should have known that no needy one ever remained destitute then. But so great was the grief that as far as Naomi was concerned, the picture couldn't have been blacker.

Of course Naomi had cause to weep. Jesus Himself wept. Paul

reminds us that we do sorrow, but not "as others which have no hope" (I Thessalonians 4:13). For Naomi the tears came for the wrong reasons. In fact, she cried the hardest when she was at the entrance to the very village that Micah prophesied would be the birthplace of the Messiah. The immensity of what God was doing through the badly underrated girl at her side passed her completely by, and she stood dissolved in tears on the threshold of a new life.

We've all experienced the forlorn feeling of being alone in our sorrow—and found later that God was nearer than we ever suspected. "My God, my God, why hast thou forsaken me?" (Psalms 22:1) cried David in one breath, and with the next, "I will fear no evil, for thou art with me . . ." (22:4). The anguish was real. No one could have convinced David otherwise at the moment, but when the pain was over and the healing had come, he would have been the first to testify that God had been there all the time.

It's the nature of loneliness—this distorted view, or rather this blindness. One wonders if Naomi ever did anything but enumerate her miseries to her long-suffering companion on the weary journey back to Bethlehem. The home she'd once had, the ease, the honor, the good husband, fine sons, and, finally, every detail of the latters' lives from the first tooth to final illness. Indeed, for all Naomi knew, she did return empty—empty of all but memories. Resigned to a life of loneliness from now on, she had begun to cling to her sorrow as though *that* gave her some status—at least it was a ready topic of conversation that she could belabor again and again.

Are we ever so preoccupied with our grief and loneliness that we don't recognize the Ruths at our sides? Perhaps she's there in very unprepossessing form—someone we may have never valued when things went well with us. God has His ministering spirits where we least expect to find them, even where we *can't* find them, and we learn only later that our lives have been touched by one of these "angels unawares."

Even as the lonely often fail to recognize the help at hand, so they fail to recognize their own inner resources. Naomi had surrendered her own self-esteem as though that were a necessary consequence of the loss of husband, sons, and possessions. Feeling worthy neither of God's intervening kindness nor of her daughter-in-law's love, how could she have a sense of self-worth? Surely she'd hit an all-time low in the art of self-isolation. This can become a habit, an automatic reflex in defeat, yet it is a form of pride in reverse. Afraid to fight back in the face of tragedy for fear of losing again, we adopt the ultimate excuse for ourselves by blaming it all on "the way the ball bounces." There's no use trying because *nothing* ever works out right for *me* anyway." Naomi had reached this point. "Call me Mara—the Lord has dealt bitterly with me. It's not *my* fault . . . and of course I can't fight *Him,* so . . . what's the use?"

And Ruth. Her very name means *friend of God.* Who could be totally desolate with such a friend? That He was a comparatively new friend, too, was perhaps to her advantage. The freshness of first encounter was still there. It's often the new Christian who copes best with trial. There's that simple expectancy that God can and will surely do what is needful, since He has just demonstrated His great power in the miracle of new birth. To the newly converted nothing seems too hard. This beautiful relationship with Naomi's God had relieved the bitterness of loss for Ruth, had eased the weary journey for her, and now would see her through the difficult period of adjustment to a new home and people. Instead of coming back feeling empty, Ruth walked into the town of Bethlehem in company with an invincible Friend.

The bereaved young widow was rich in other ways. In a culture where women rarely moved beyond the sheltering framework of home and family and local friendships, Ruth wasn't afraid to step out of the old context and try something new. That it was with Naomi's God that she went mitigated the terror, but it was a very big step, nevertheless, that Ruth took when she turned her back on all that was familiar. Fear can be the paralyzing factor that locks the lonely forever within a sterile life pattern. Fierce loyalty to a place—or a memory—isn't always God's perfect way. Sometimes economic necessity will even force one into a new realm of life that would never have been attempted otherwise. With Ruth it was a matter of choice, which makes her doubly admirable.

The two women had arrived at Bethlehem just at barley harvest. It couldn't have taken Ruth long to put this fact to work for her and her mother-in-law. Food they needed. Nothing debatable about that. And with energy and enthusiasm Ruth headed for the likeliest field to glean. It highlights another characteristic of this unusual young woman: the ability to recognize opportunity when it came knocking. Certainly those waiting handfuls didn't require any great talent to gather. They were just *there*, for the taking, by whoever had the gumption to go and get them. The choice was hers. Either she could stay home and lament, or she could go and help herself. All the handfuls in the world left on purpose by a generous Boaz wouldn't have done her any good if she hadn't recognized the opportunity available in the neighboring fields.

Ruth didn't underestimate her resources. It was a quality that contrasted with the sense of worthlessness that left her mother-in-law prostrated. Early in her spiritual experience Ruth was learning that it was possible to be "troubled on every side, yet not distressed; . . . perplexed, but not in despair; Persecuted, but not forsaken; cast down, but not destroyed" (2 Corinthians 4:8, 9). She learned the reassuring fact that God supplies according to the *need.* A healthy young body Ruth had. Add to that that it was barley harvest. No need for Elijah's ravens to feed these two. Action was part of God's healing therapy and Ruth pitched in with a will.

Even old Naomi wasn't as empty as she imagined. She carried something back to Bethlehem which she could never lose, and it was her unique contribution to this winning combination. No one who keeps an unblemished good name as Naomi had goes empty-handed. She had given that name by way of marriage to Ruth, and without it Ruth would never have won her husband or her place in history. So each, in her own way, contributed her part to the working of God's plan.

The lonely and bereaved often don't have the courage or emotional reserves to plan intelligently for the future. The best they can manage is a day-by-day acceptance of the way that they must go. When Ruth woke up that first morning in a strange town, she wasn't faced with the next 365 friendless and hungry days all at once. There was no way that that first dawn could cancel out the rancor of generations or ten years of poverty. On the contrary, it was the necessities of *that day* she faced. It meant recognizing that day's need for food and deliberately turning her feet in the direction of the ripe fields. It meant gathering sufficient for one day and all the while facing with gracious mien the speculative glances of her fellow workers. The next day she set out again to gather for that day's need . . . .

Because Ruth wasn't unrealistically ambitious or demanding, there was no chance to be disappointed. Having come to Bethlehem materially "empty," there was no way to go but up anyway. It wasn't by any means an attitude that negated the hope that tomorrow would be better, only that today could be coped with if taken a moment at a time. Surely Ruth's hope wasn't in her circumstances anyway. There wasn't any earthly reason that she knew of that those would ever change. But she had reason to hope in the God of Israel. "Why art thou cast down, O my soul?" David asked himself. ". . . Hope thou in God" (Psalms 42:5). And with this healthy, happy hope before her, Ruth gleaned each day's blessing in the fields of Boaz . . . .

Barley harvest came and went—and wheat harvest. Every day Ruth turned her feet toward Boaz's fields and bent her back to the work she had to do. No demands on the future. Nightly thanks for the day's mercies. What a life. And still her reputation flourished. "A good name is more to be desired than riches" (Proverbs 22:1). Ruth was fast becoming one of the richest girls in town.

Of course there's more to the story. Ruth continued trusting and Naomi continued scheming. Let's give Naomi the benefit of the doubt and call it *divine* scheming. But the real burden of proof lay with Ruth. That little Moabite stranger who refused to be lonely won over not only Boaz but every last elder in the city gates. The finest wedding congratulation they could think of to bestow on the happy bridegroom was to compare his prize to Rachel and Leah, the mothers of Israel. And the women who'd almost looked through and around and over Ruth when she'd first arrived? For Naomi they could think of no greater blessing when her grandson was laid in her arms than, "Your daughter-in-law who loves you so is better than seven sons."

Ruth was home at last.

Anna B. Mow

Say "Yes" to Life

Anna B. Mow and her husband, Baxter, were missionaries in India for almost twenty years. Since returning to the States, she has been a seminary professor, leader of Spiritual Life Retreats, author of ten books, and grandmother of nineteen. Long before the ministry became a feminist issue, Anna Mow was ordained by the Church of the Brethren. An octogenarian activist, she travels extensively, speaking, leading Holy Land tours, and she still finds time to write. Her latest book is *Find Your Own Faith.*

Testing! Testing!

Commitment to Christ is spontaneous when our attention is wholly upon Him as it is in a high and holy hour of worship. The laboratory, however, for this new life is in the world around us. It is first of all in the home, then in any other close relationships in which we are involved in our daily living. No matter how difficult the problem, how unhappy the situation, a Christlike way must be found to meet it. This way may not always be easy. Jesus went on to the Cross because that was the only way God could reveal His great love to the world. As He revealed the Father we must live to reveal His life and love.

Several months ago I was greatly burdened for a friend who faced a seemingly hopeless situation. I knew she had gone to a Spiritual Life Retreat. I hoped she could see her situation as Christ saw it, whatever that was. I still feel the touch of God's hand of love as I think of her letter: "What did God do for me at the Retreat? I went asking Him for courage to get out of this heartbreaking mess. I argued with God because I wanted out. I spent much time in the Prayer Room, always asking for courage to leave. He wanted to give me courage and strength to stay. I was assured that His grace is sufficient if I put myself aside. To accept God's grace makes me feel good; to appropriate it makes me want to make others feel good. I find His grace is not full without both—acceptance and appropriation. God has been so good to me I could not bolt this offer from Him."

In reading the Letter to the Ephesians, one's mind and spirit are stretched by the magnitude of the great thoughts presented: Jesus as the center and culmination of history; the power of God available to us for any situation in individual or group experience; the Christ who dwells in our hearts and also is the head of the church which is His body on earth.

One feels overawed with religious joy with these wonderful thoughts until the finger of the Spirit hunts around for sore spots to see if we are really appropriating what He offers to us. "Woman, how do you relate to your husband?" "Man, how do you love your wife?" "Parents, are you carrying your responsibility in training your children so they are capable of knowing God?" "Children, do you obey your parents in the Lord?" "Servants and masters, what is your relationship to one another?" (Management and labor, is your relationship in harmony with your worship on Sunday?)

The general principle to apply to all these relationships is stated in Ephesians 5:21—"Be submissive to one another out of reverence for Christ" (MLB). I have just seen a woman who walks in this kind of reverence. She was my hostess for several days. She seemed to have an inner holy quiet which reached out to everyone. It did not separate her from others. It made her available. Interruptions didn't bother her. It was hard to believe that she was once a frustrated woman full of anxiety. Now she goes through the frustrations of the day remembering her Lord whom she represents to everyone who crosses her path. With all this she has a keen sense of humor and a sweet dignity.

"Being submissive to one another" is an attitude usually disdained by Christians as it is by others. Much less is it ever considered any kind of a spiritual law. If we really understood the power of Christ's life we would be less afraid of this idea which is the basic principle of love.

Paul was talking about the same thing when he wrote to the Philippians who were having some troubles among themselves: "If, therefore, in relationship with Christ there is any encouragement, if there is any persuasive appeal of love, if there is any fellowship in the Spirit, if any deep-felt affections and sympathies, then make my joy complete by your mutual identity of purpose, your common object of love, your fellowship of feeling and your harmonious thinking. You will not act from factional motives or out of vanity, but with humble-mindedness each will regard the other superior to himself; neither will each be looking out only for his own interests, but also for those of others.

"Let this mind be in you, which was also in Christ Jesus, who, though existing in the form of God, did not consider His equality with God something to cling to, but emptied Himself as He took on the form of a servant and became like human beings. So, recognized in looks as a human being, He humbled Himself and lived obediently to the extreme of death; yes, death by the cross" (Philippians 2:1–8 MLB).

We are inclined to shy away and say, "Yes, but that was Jesus." We who follow Jesus must face the fact of the life of Mahatma Gandhi. He took the law of love and humble service seriously. He submitted himself completely to the welfare of his nation as well as to the lowliest of those he met. He paid no attention to those who told him this way of love would not work in a world like this. It did work and his nation won her freedom. When Gandhi died, humanity lowered its flag. Senator Vandenberg said, "Gandhi made humility and truth more powerful than empires." We said this even more about Jesus but we didn't really believe it.

This spiritual law of selflessness is the key to the entrance of the kingdom of heaven: "Blessed are they who sense spiritual poverty, for theirs is the kingdom of heaven" (Matthew 5:3, 5 MLB). This is the way this spiritual law is stated in its relationship to God. But in relation to people the same quality of life is called *meekness or gentleness.* "Blessed are the gentle (the meek) for they shall inherit the earth." The world insistently misinterprets meekness and gentleness. It is never weakness, it is always strength. Some who know call them "The Terrible Meek." It is a strength that physical power cannot fathom or threaten. It is not to be passive, to be pushed around, to cringe in fear. One good look at Jesus should correct that error. Jesus was crucified, but He was never pushed around. He was crowned with thorns, but He was not browbeaten. He never cringed, He never lost His dignity, He was never frightened. Pilate, the governor of the state, with all his military power, was the frightened one. And history says that Jesus was not tried before

Pilate, but Pilate was on trial before Jesus.

Some years ago on the first day of a summer retreat a handsome Negro minister rose to tell his greatest need. His head hung low as he said haltingly, "I am a broken man. I have no courage to go on. Even among ministers of the Gospel I don't know whether to be conscious of Christ or of my color." For two weeks he shared fully in a fellowship in Christ. On the last day he stood up with his head held high and said, "I am a new man in Christ Jesus. I can go out from this place and take anything that can happen to me."

On the first day this brother felt humiliated but he was not humble. On the last day when he held his head high with the dignity any man can have in Christ Jesus, he was truly humble, for now he was no longer thinking of himself. Such are the poor in spirit, rich in His Spirit. Such are the meek, strong with gracious dignity because their security is in that which cannot be hurt or shaken.

This is the quality of "being submissive to one another out of reverence for Christ." The Apostle Paul saw this loving submission to the welfare of another as the outstanding characteristic of motherhood. When his heart was broken over the Galatian Christians who so quickly changed their allegiance from Christ to another gospel he cried out to them, "My children, over whom I once more suffer birthpains until Christ is formed within you" (Galatians 4:19 MLB). Only in terms of selfless creative motherhood could he express his concern.

Paul took it for granted that mothers would understand what he was trying to say about a quality of life in Christ which would be evident in every relationship. So he said to the women first as wives, "Wives, be submissive to your husbands as to the Lord." This has nothing to do with being a "doormat." It has nothing to do with unwilling or rebellious submission to an intolerable situation. There is no room for self-pity because all the energies of a giving love are turned creatively toward the highest well-being of the loved one. This love has courage, patience, hope because of a knowledge of Christ's power available for appropriation in any need.

Those who do not know the power of this giving love are possessed by the great American fear of being "walked over," "henpecked," or being made a "doormat." We have such a fear of the word "obey" that we have unconscious fears of obeying God. This is a fear born from self-interest. Self-interest breeds the very results that it is guarding against. It short circuits real love every time.

Many people do not know that there is a *giving love.* A movie star divorced her fourth husband with this explanation for her numerous marriages: "Four marriages make me seem much worse than I am but that's because I married every man I fell in love with. Love is great. So are men. It's marriage I'm a little disappointed in." (She recently divorced her fifth!)

Real love is not getting, but giving. With reverence I remember a precious little woman who through the years caused me to marvel at her courage in a difficult situation. Her husband is naturally kind and generous, but when drunk he is cruel. She learned to keep quiet, to avoid the things which irritated. She endured because she loved him dearly in spite of his weakness. She also remembered his childhood and adult experiences with unloving church members which caused him to shy away from the church. She knew about his deep spiritual longings. So she has waited with patience. At last, the waiting is bringing results. She has no more need to fear her husband. Recently she said to me, "I consider my marriage a success; I have made my husband happy."

Mothers and wives have no corner on this love market. Giving love is for husbands, too. Some years ago my brother was waiting to become a grandfather. He had almost lost his wife when their daughter Harriett was born. Now Harriett was to have her first child and two weeks had passed since the designated date for the birth. I found my brother pacing the floor. I came up behind him and said, "William, I found it much more difficult to become a grandmother than to become a mother." William answered, "Yes, that's when a woman finds out what a man goes through."

The fact is that Paul wrote more in the fifth chapter of Ephesians for the husbands than for the wives: "Husbands, love your wives, even as Christ loved the Church and gave Himself for her." I speak for all women when I say that any woman would be willing to be a doormat for a man who loved her like that!

It must be understood that this kind of love does not mean *domination* of either one over the other. One man said, "My wife and I are one. I'm the one." In many cases the wife is the guilty one. For a man or a woman to dominate or succumb is an entirely different matter from the healthy chosen submission to another that Paul discusses. The Christian admonition cannot mean domination because Christ never dominates anyone. He *draws* us with His great love.

"Perfect love casts out fear" so neither one feels compelled to protect himself from the other. With such Christ-love in the human relationship even competition becomes irrelevant. We become competitive when we feel our own personalities being threatened by another. The competitive spirit is melted away by giving love. Only through giving love can there be fulfillment in this closest of human relationships.

Two can become one only through this giving love. For those who find this kind of love, life has a great surprise package: the individual personality is not obliterated. Each has a new freedom to be himself. The freedom for fulfillment found in the commitment to Christ is now accentuated in the closest human relationship.

Historically, there is only one thing wrong with "Wives, obey your husbands." Husbands have used this order on their wives. This admonition is for the wives, and they must *choose* it, or it has no spiritual value or power. The admonition for the husbands is, "Love your wife as Christ loved the church." Each to his own personal admonition.

However, the husband is the head of the wife "as Christ is the head of the church." Obviously this does not mean that he can *demand* this headship on "scriptural grounds" even though it has been quoted thus through long years of church history. The clue to the significance of this *headship* I found in a report of a conference on Christian marriage which was held in Woudschouten by the Dutch Reformed Church in July, 1952. They asked the next question which I stupidly didn't think of doing before: "How is Christ the head of the Church?"

The answer to that question is quite clear: "Whoever among you wants to be great must be your minister and whoever would be first shall be your servant; just as the Son of Man did not come to be served but to serve, and to give His life a ransom for many" (Matthew 20:26–28 MLB). Christ is the head of the church by being the servant of the church. Therefore, if the husband is the head of his wife as Christ is the head of the church, *he is the servant* of his wife *as Christ is the servant* of the church.

So everyone who loves is a servant. The circle is complete. In

Christ's life-giving, serving love for us we have the real definition of the spiritual law for human relationships: "Be submissive to one another out of reverence for Christ."

For Further Study

Compare other references to Christian home relationships.

1 Corinthians 7
Colossians 3:18–25
1 Peter 2:18–3:7

Use your home as a laboratory for testing out "giving love."

Edith Schaeffer

What Is a Family?

Edith Schaeffer, along with her remarkable family, founded L'Abri, the famous Christian community in Switzerland, where she demonstrates day-by-day Kingdom hospitality and a profoundly creative understanding of relationships. She not only encourages the prodigious talents of her husband, Dr. Francis Schaeffer, she is a popular individualist, author, speaker, and counselor.

A Museum of Memories

Smoke curling up towards the autumn blue sky drifts to your nostrils, "Mmm. The burning of leaves always takes me back to when I was nine and used to shuffle through the maple leaves curling up in yellow and brown drifts on our lawn—Dad raking them, Mother helping—a warm, happy feeling of preparation for the winter. Mother saying, 'These ashes will be so wonderful for the rose beds,' and Dad asking, 'Did I hear you say not to forget to remind you to get the apple pie out of the oven? I think it's time now.' Just the *smell* of that smoke brings back the whole period of my childhood I loved best."

"Fresh coconut, mmm, what a lovely, wet, crisp taste. This flavor always brings back the beach at Alassio, where the one thing cheap enough for us to buy each day was the coconut cut in slices and carried by the beach vendors in bowls of water. I feel the sand, the spray of salt sea in my face, and remember the call, 'Come on in and jump these next waves!'—'Soon as I finish my coconut!' What an amazing thing *taste* can do to you!"

"OOOwwwooo—listen to that deep-throated sound of the boat whistle—my favorite noise in the world. It brings back the whole feeling of the throb-throb of engines starting, of the bustle of a ship setting sail across the ocean, the sadness of leaving, the excitement of going, the curiosity of what the first dinner would be like, the unpacking to settle in for the period of suspended time between two continents—the feel of hot sun on the deck, the marvel of water splitting apart in white froth as the midnight moon lights up the wake and one feels alone in such a different way, hung out over the sea on the upper prow of the ship. Just the wwwOOOooo of the whistle brings it all back. Boat whistles! What a string of things that *noise* does to me."

"Satin, what a feeling between the fingers. I remember the satin binding of my first blanket. How old would that memory be? The feel of satin always brings back the contented sensation of being tucked in bed, of the satin binding under my chin and reassuringly felt between my fingers. The 'lovey" blanket of my childhood and strings of nights of security. Satin brings it all back." *Feels* are like that. The rough tongue of a cat brings back not just the ginger cat of our old Cape Cod cottage, but the whole summer we were there—the treks to the beach past the graveyard, the heaviness of pushing two two-year-olds in one pram, the picnics on the beach, and the mice running along the skirting boards. A cat's rough tongue, the feel of it! What an amazing thing is *feel!*

Music is incredible. Sudden strains of the wedding march, or the Handel played at other weddings you've been to, and the whole wedding comes back—the panic of the missing flowers, the disappointing color of the cake's icing, the beauty of the whole ceremony, the loveliness of the bride, and the depth of emotions. A few strains of music, just that particular music, and it all floods back. The first song your mother ever sang to you, the first symphony you ever went to, the popular song that everyone was humming when you were thirteen—it isn't just the music that you "put into a slot" timewise when you hear it, but it is the flood of related experiences that come back to be relived. Memories with a sudden searchlight of music focused into the present.

Memory! What a gift of God. And what a tragedy at times. Memory can be of horrible things one wants to forget, coming at times like a nightmare bringing trembling and horror, or memory can be of wonderful things one enjoys living and reliving. Memory can bring sudden understanding later in life when things suddenly fall into place and you realize what was happening, and memory can give courage to go on—just when it is needed. Memory can quiet one in time of turmoil or can transport one out of the danger of being plunged into something false. Memory can suddenly become so vivid as to stop a person from doing something wrong—because of the unmistakable contrast being flashed on the screen of the mind—and memory can cause someone to be compassionate to another in need, whose need would not have been noticed had it not been linked in the mind's picture with a deep experience in the past which prepared an understanding.

A museum has a selection of things worth preserving. There are art museums, natural-history museums, maritime museums, and those preserving documents of a variety of kinds. There are period-furniture museums, those with jewelry from different periods of history, or with rare Chinese pottery. Some cities are a museum in themselves, like Florence in Italy, where the buildings, gates, doors of churches, towers, and outdoor statues make walking at any time of the day or night a time of exclaiming over marble, intricate carvings, wonderful architecture, sudden vistas with a bridge showing up between angles of buildings, and the moon sliding around an ancient tower. Not as old, but still with as much history behind it, is Salem, Massachusetts, with not only a collection of museums, but houses furnished with the possessions of four generations, and old Chestnut Street with its Early American houses and lovely old trees preserving the flavor of another period of history. Had someone not had the idea of selecting and putting things together in some sort of order, much of past history would be lost as far as the vividness of reality given by the collections of things in museums.

What is a family meant to be? Among other things, I personally have always felt it is meant to be a *museum of memories*—collections of carefully preserved memories and a realization that day-by-day memories are being chosen for our museum. Someone in the family—one who is happily making it his or her career, or both parents, perhaps a grandparent or two, aunts and uncles, older brothers and sisters—at least one person needs to be conscious that memories are important, and that time can be made to have double value by recognizing that what is done today will be tomorrow's memory.

Memories (not all of them, but *some* of them) should be planned with the same careful kind of planning one would give to designing a museum. A family life in retrospect should be a museum of diverse and greatly varied memories, with a unity that makes the grouping of people involved share at least many if not all the overlapping memories. Memories don't need to be just a thing of chance collection, but can have some measure of planning. Of course, no one can plan an hour, a day, a week, a month, or a year without saying and meaning that, "Lord willing," we will do thus and so. The Bible makes this very strong: "Go to now, ye that say, To day or to morrow we will go into such a city, and continue there a year, and buy and sell, and get gain: Whereas ye know not what shall be on the morrow. For what is your life? It is even a vapour, that appeareth for a little time, and then vanisheth away. For that ye ought to say, If the Lord will, we shall live, and do this, or that" (James 4:13–15).

This is a basic teaching of the Bible to those of us who are the people of God. We must always remember within ourselves and teach our children that in any plan we should not only *say,* "Lord willing," but mean it. We should believe and teach our children that *only* God can always keep His promises and make plans that cannot be broken or suddenly changed. We can say, "I will do that and go thus far and no farther." We can promise, "I will be there tomorrow and make such and such for you." But—we may be in a hospital by that time—or be forced to fly around the world to meet an emergency—or be interrupted or hindered in a thousand possible ways. As we go on to think of planned memories, it is with the need of always saying, "Lord willing," and actually praying, "Please show me, Lord, whether this is Your will or not."

With that being laid down as an accepted and understood condition, memories ought to be planned, memories ought to be chosen, memories ought to be put in the budget, memories ought to be recognized and given the proper amount of time, memories ought to be protected, memories ought not to be wasted, and memories ought to be passed down to the next generation.

How can memories be planned? First of all, as a new family starts, it is good to carry on *old* traditions and to start some *new* traditions of your own. What kind of traditions? Birthdays should be celebrated in some special way. Each family can have its own traditions woven into the remembering of a birthday. Perhaps everyone screams, "Happy Birthday!" first thing in the morning, or the birthday person is served breakfast in bed . . . .

There is discussion among Christians as to how Christmas should be celebrated and what sort of traditions should be handed down. It seems to me that God makes this clear to us in Romans 14:5,

6—which strongly says that there are some who place one day above another in importance, and that it is up to the individuals as to whether they regard certain days as special or not. There is room for individual differences, as long as we do what we do "unto the Lord" in the way we regard the day . . . .

There is something about saying, "We *always* do this," which helps to keep the years together. Time is such an elusive thing that if we keep on meaning to do something interesting, but never doing it, year would follow year with no special thoughtfulness being expressed in making gifts, surprises, charming table settings, and familiar, favorite food. It is important to have certain times when you look at the calendar and say, "Oh, yes, time for the geranium plants to be put in the window box!"—"Oh, look at the date; we'd better get ready for our traditional treasure hunt."—"I've got a wow-ee idea for Christmas stocking tops this year . . . ."

And whether a person adopts children, adopts grandparents in the old-folks' home, or adopts someone in a hospital ward, no one needs to be without someone to care for on dates ticked off on the calendar as special for some reason.

How do you choose a memory? First there is the choice that involves *time*, but no money . . . . For years the ten-year-old and the three- and five-year-old will remember the bubbles of excitement that came when Mother and Daddy said, "We have finished the doctor's appointment and we could take the next train [or drive home on the expressway as fast as possible], but we have decided to turn off and go to the zoo [or the aquarium or the birdhouse in the park]. We didn't plan to do this, but we thought it would be fun for all of us." The bubble of excitement, the thrill that comes in being loved and considered important, the reality of discovering that our mother and father really like to be together with us, the highlighted enjoyment of whatever it is you decide to do, will make it a stronger, longer-lasting and more vivid memory than even the planned days off could ever be. The memory multiplies the use of those hours into hundreds of hours!

When you choose a memory in this way, you are choosing to lose hours of time—in order to keep them! A family should have a whole museum of memories gathered through the years—of moments when the choice has been to go ahead and lose a couple of hours in order to save them . . . .

If you wait "until you are older" or "for a more convenient time," the time of life—which is like a river flowing under a bridge—will all be gone, and the "right time" will have passed under the bridge along with the rest of time! Memories must take time, and the *choice* of a memory always means that a negative choice is made not to use the time another way. We are finite, and in our finiteness and limitedness we can never choose to do something without choosing not to do something else . . . .

There must be some times of choosing memories very consciously or your family museum will be an empty, echoing building waiting for new acquisitions which you will never have time to acquire. This is because *people* are involved in the memories, and the togetherness only lasts a certain length of time. The together-as-a-family memories are limited as to "gathering time."

"How romantic! Children don't remember things all that early." Do I hear you objecting? People differ in the things they remember and as to the age they were when they started collecting memories. For example, I only lived in China until I was five years old, yet I have so very many strong memories—memories of being taught how to scoop the rice into my mouth and pack it with chopsticks at one side of my cheeks while tea could be sipped down the other side from the lovely cups without handles, not disturbing a grain of rice! I remember the anxious, loving faces of my dear Chinese friends teaching me this, and the children I had been playing with before, running in for that particular meal. I remember my lessons in bargaining with the vendors who came to the door, and the Chinese cook and gatekeeper of the compound who were so delighted not only because I spoke perfect Chinese, but knew how to get the price down! I remember the sad shock of the realities of human beings' ways of cheating and stealing—when my beautiful kite was flying high, but another kite cleverly maneuvered from the street side of the wall pulled down my kite and someone cut the string, so that I stood dismayed with my empty string, disillusioned for the first time! I have hundreds of memories which must have been collected before I was five.

Memories not chosen, but given day by day, are also being collected. Is a slap in the face a first memory? Or is it the memory of Mommy still being there when the early streaks of dawn starting to come through the curtains startle you into seeing that "Mommy has been up all night because I had the croup. She didn't go to bed at all. Oh, Mommy!" You can't choose the first memory; you can't regulate what will be remembered and what will be forgotten. If there are enough lovely memories, and if there are apologies for making really wrong choices, then the museum will have a good balance and a nonromantic reality of what life is like.

Of course, there will also be memories of flare-ups in the family. "Daddy is awfully mad right now!" can be said by a four-year-old without any tragic results. "Mommy is in a bad humor; I'm going to stay in here till she feels better!" will not harm any child. The reality of the ups and downs of dispositions, of people's tempers or of their mistakes and actual sins, does not tear apart the museum of memories, nor does it have to tear up the home or split the family. A realistic facing of the imperfections, faults, weaknesses, blind spots, and sins of each other in the family, although it will never be a complete facing of the whole person, will be a measure of understanding the whole person which will give a preparation for the future. If every fault, weakness, imperfection, blind spot, or sin was able to be *hidden* from each other, the relationships and the reality of having lived together as a family would be a hypocritical farce! To succeed in hiding everything but the good things in the years of living together, would be like a married couple never undressing in front of each other, going to bed clothed, never seeing each other naked, as far as the physical "knowing" of each other goes . . . .

In some ways a family ought to be a mutual-admiration society . . . . We need to give compliments, praise each other, point out the things we admire and love. Children need to be praised for doing as well as they can, even if their marks are not the highest. To teach parents to never praise, but always to set the goal higher, is to give children a horrible childhood of never feeling they have succeeded in pleasing anyone. Praise is needed badly, and the Bible sets forth the principle of kindness to each other in this area, too—praise and thankfulness and expression of appreciation are meant to be given to each other as well as to God. Therefore, before speaking of the fact that our memories will contain upsetting times which we lived through, it is important to set forth the strong fact of our need for reassurance time after time, and the pleading with each other not to "destroy" each other by constantly dwelling on the weaknesses (with a virtuous feeling of being honest or realistic or nonhypocritical). One can carry too far this pointing out or recognizing or talking about faults. That is called by a good old-fashioned word—*nagging.* A parent can nag a child, a child can nag a parent, a brother can nag a sister, a sister can nag a brother, a husband can nag a wife, a wife can nag a husband, and we could go on with the whole list of life's possible relationships. To recognize each other's good points and to have the family really admire each other is a basic source of stability in our lives. But to recognize each other's weaknesses and to speak of things that happened in the past which were a result of those weaknesses, is not harmful if kept in some sort of balance. The museum of memories will have memories not planned, not chosen, and some of them will be good ones—and some will be of flare-ups, arguments, disappointments, as well as of sicknesses, accidents, and tragedies.

Some family "skeletons," however, can be memories which will help in the next generation's married lives. THINGS TO AVOID also belong in a collection of helpful memories. My children will always remember my reaction to frustration or anger of a certain intensity. When my adrenaline flows, my reaction is to try to get more done in the next hours than any human being could do. My hands move faster, my whole body goes into high gear, and I speed up like a car passing the speed limits—the needle swerves and hits the highest point! What has set me off? Some criticism or disparaging remark: "Why haven't you done . . . ?"—whatever it might be. "What have you been doing all this time?" Rather than sensibly pointing out what has taken my time (and what has been accomplished), I react (I could say react*ed*, but to be honest I don't suppose I have ever stopped) by zooming into high gear and for the next few hours doing ten times more than I should, whether it is washing windows, taking the curtains down to wash them, cleaning out cupboards, doing piles of washing and ironing, or whatever . . . .

Your museum of memories will not all be made up of chosen memories and understanding the better use of time, but there will be both good and disturbing memories which will help your children to have a realistic understanding of human beings, of life in a fallen world where sin continues to spoil things, and of the fact that there can be a rebuilding after an "earthquake," and that it is worth it all to go back and make a new start.

"How many times shall we forgive?" Jesus is asked. "Shall it be seven times?" asks Peter (*see* Matthew 18:21, 22). *Shall we forgive each other seven times?*—Peter wants to know as practical preparation for knowing when to say, "Okay, this is the last time." And the answer of Jesus comes to Peter and to us, "Jesus saith unto him, I say not unto thee, Until seven times: but, Until seventy times seven." And when we couple that with what Jesus taught us to ask God in day-by-day prayer, "Forgive us our trespasses as we forgive those who trespass against us," it becomes very sobering, even frightening. Jesus is saying something real when He goes on to say, "For if ye forgive men their trespasses, your heavenly Father will also forgive you: But if ye forgive not men their trespasses, neither will your Father forgive your trespasses" (*see* Matthew 6:12, 14, 15). "Put on therefore . . . [a heart of compassion], kindness, humbleness of mind, meekness, longsuffering; Forbearing one another, and forgiving one another, if any man have a quarrel against any: even as Christ forgave you, so also do ye" (Colossians 3:12, 13). This is talking about relationships within the family, as well as with other people. God means us to pay attention to His warnings. There is meant to be, in our dealings with each other, a consideration of what He has done for us. Who of us is so perfect as to stand in condemnation and judgment and say, "I won't forgive," to a child or to a husband or wife or to brothers or sisters or to grandparents or aunts or uncles? Forgiveness is meant to be *experienced* in a two-way manner in a family, and memories should contain memories of forgiveness. If the weakness, fault, mistake, or sin has never been acknowledged or noticed, then the forgiveness cannot be given or become a reality.

Memories ought to be put in the budget. This is a sentence to underline in red ink in your mind. How do you put memories in your budget? Of course it involves a choice, but this time it is a choice in which the spending of money must be definitely faced. You have a little fund or box or an envelope in which you have tucked away bits of saving when you have economized, or when birthday presents have been given to you. Perhaps you have in mind a few possibilities of what you want to use it for—you could get a rug for that old stained linoleum floor on your sewing-room office or new linoleum for the kitchen or even a new winter coat.

Then you get the Music Festival programs for the summer and fall, and notice that there is to be an unusual concert—the Philharmonic Symphony soloists playing as a quintet of strings at Castle Chillon. (It depends on where you live in the world, but I have to use illustrations of my own experience.) The question comes to you and to me: "What is more important, the rug, my linoleum, or memories that will last a lifetime for my children and grandchildren? How long do we have before war makes concerts an impossibility? How long do we have before the family circle will be broken?" And the determination comes—to choose seats, to send off a letter for reservations, to pay the staggering amount! Are you crazy? You go off with little girls dressed in their last year's family-reunion dresses, with adults dressed up and happy, looking forward to being transported into Bach's, Beethoven's, and Brahms's world, being carried off into another century as we all enter the castle . . . . Will the adults of the family ever forget the evening? Will the children? Who could forget the full moon behind the Castle Chillon, with floodlights illuminating the old moss-covered rocks? Who could forget crossing the covered bridge and peering over to see the dark water rippling below, imagining the days of captive prisoners and the deep intrigue centering in this very place? Who could forget the togetherness of sharing such an experience on the various levels on which it has been shared? What has the money been spent for? Anything tangible? *Memories.* Memories which cannot be taken away from any person who has made up the family group that night, memories which will come back to lull each one to sleep during some restless night of tossing with worries of one kind or another. Memories help to sort out the reality of what God has given us in beauty, to share horizontally in our capacity for enjoyment. Memories help children to realize the contrast of what they were being lured into with promises of "fun," when the fun includes drugs and the dangerous spoiling of the tomorrows with ugly hangovers of some kind. An evening like the one at Chillon, once in memory's museum, is a tremendous protection against false judgments as to what a great evening is like. "The blessing of the Lord, it maketh rich, and he addeth no sorrow with it" (Proverbs 10:22). How better can you really teach children what this means—than by spending money for memories which illustrate this fact? . . .

Constantly you need to think of what will last longer, with greater results, a new car or a memory! What about schedules, sleep, school, meals on time, and the usual standards of values as to how to use time day by day? There are times when memories are in danger of being *un*recognized and the time is going to be wasted or lost, with the memory uncaptured! What sorts of memories need to be recognized, protected, captured in the nick of time, before they are lost? Here are a few reminders:

"It will be after your bedtime, but, yes, you can go to the airport and say good-bye to Grandfather. You may never get to do just this again."

"There is a fantastic double rainbow. It doesn't matter whether or not supper spoils a bit. Never mind it, let's all run outside and watch until it fades."

"Mr. Q. is going to bring his slides of African jungles with him to supper tonight. Let the children stay up to see them. They can get their baths first and watch in pajamas."

"We have these little pieces of smoked glass ready to look at the eclipse of the sun. You can all wait for it; never mind the music lesson this time."

"The parade is going right by the house. We'll have sandwiches and ice-cream cones ready and eat them outside so we won't miss it—then save for tomorrow our meal that was ready."

"It's Grandmother's birthday party and we may never have this kind of togetherness again. Let's take Fiona wrapped up in blankets, but give her the antibiotic first. She can lie on the couch, and I don't think it will hurt her."

"It doesn't matter if *we are* all alone. The extra time it takes to put a candle and this African violet on the tray will make a memory of our midnight snack in bed."

"Yes, I do think the children should be allowed to take flowers to Grandmother's bed and put them around her body. Quite the opposite from being shattering, it will help them understand death—and the body being here while the person has gone to heaven—more vividly than anything else. The memory will be tremendously important. Of course, let them pick flowers and go in that room two at a time. Now—you can't decide later."

"Take someone along to take care of little Matthew outside the hospital, after he has had his peek through the nursery window at his baby sister. It takes one extra person's time, but has a value you couldn't assess. Even if he can't go inside for the length of time his father can, the few moments will be a memory all his life."

What is a family? Oh, what *is* a family?—*a museum of memories.*

"What do *you* do? You're just a housewife and slave, aren't you? A nursemaid to a bunch of kids?"—"No, I have a fantastic job, a terrific career. I am a curator in a museum—a museum of memories!"

"You're tied down by a whole family. What a bore! Don't you wish you could get away with the fellows for a real good time?"—"No, I can't waste my time that way. I'm a collector, you see. I have to spend my time collecting, whenever I'm not tied up in work. I am collecting memories for our family museum!"

Mrs. Norman Vincent Peale

The Adventure of Being a Wife

Ruth Peale, coeditor of *Guideposts* magazine, has been acknowledged for her contributions as a leader and administrator of many Christian organizations.

Having many times heard the cry, "What can I do, I'm just a housewife," Mrs. Peale encourages women to recognize that, as wives, they can be the ones to set the emotional climates in their homes and thereby be powerful forces in the lives of their family members.

Who's the Optimist in Your House?

It was one of those isn't-it-a-small-world coincidences. I was on my way to Chicago to join Norman, who had a speaking engagement there. The woman who happened to sit beside me in the airplane was a stranger. But when we identified ourselves, it turned out that during her visit to New York she had attended a service at the Marble Church and had heard Norman preach.

"Oh," she cried, "it was such a practical sermon. I came to church feeling dispirited and depressed, and I went away feeling like a new woman. I just wish my husband could have heard that sermon. He certainly could use a lift."

"What's the problem?" I asked her. "What's bothering your husband?"

She shook her head resignedly. "Everything bothers him! The state of the world bothers him. The state of his health bothers him. His job and his finances bother him. He's the most downbeat, pessimistic man I know. Life in our house with my husband around is one long gloom."

"Well," I said, "can't you change that?"

"Me?" She looked astonished. "Why, I'm just his wife. What can I do about it?"

"Everything," I said.

"Oh, come now, Mrs. Peale," she said, half disbelieving and half indignant. "It's easy for you to talk. You're married to one of the world's great optimists. You haven't any idea of what I'm up against."

"Oh yes, I have," I answered quickly. "Every wife runs into this problem from time to time and I'm no exception. It's true that my husband is a great optimist. He believes in the goodness of life, and the goodness in people. But he has his moments of discouragement, too. And believe me, his outlook can turn quite dark. When he gets depressed, he sees only the negative side of everything. Sometimes I think he writes about positive thinking because he understands so much about negative thinking! Of course, he knows that it doesn't get him anywhere, and he can and does come out of these moods. But I consider it part of my job as a wife to understand all this, to evaluate it unemotionally, and then do something about it."

"Do something about it?" she said with surprise. "Why, all I want to do is get out of the house and leave my husband alone with his miserable thoughts and hope he will come out of it quickly."

"Oh, no," I responded in dismay. "You're taking the easy way out, and in the process you're missing a chance to make your job as a wife into an adventure."

"Well, I never heard anything like that, Mrs. Peale," my new-found friend replied. "How do you do it? I mean, how do you help your husband when he is depressed? You almost make it sound as if my husband's pessimism were my fault!"

"Maybe to some extent it is," I said. "I think the wife is the one who can set the emotional climate of the home. Basically, women are more stable emotionally than men—although most men won't admit it. Women are not so vulnerable to disappointment. They're used to soothing hurt feelings and bandaging skinned knees. Ten thousand years ago, when the hunters came back to the cave day after day empty-handed, and the sabre-toothed tiger howled outside, who do you think said, 'Don't worry; everything will be all right'? Was it the brawny caveman? It was not! It was the cavewoman, and she's been saying it ever since."

"That may be true," my companion said stubbornly. "But I still don't think you realize how contagious pessimism can be."

"No more contagious than optimism," I said. "But let's take this problem and go at it logically for a few minutes. To begin with, is there anything really seriously wrong with your husband's health or his finances?"

"No," she said. "It's all a state of mind."

"All right," I said, "let's consider your tactics. When your husband starts complaining or grumbling or finding fault with things, what's your reaction? Do you really leave the house, or what exactly do you do?"

"Usually I urge him not to be such a complainer. I tell him he's getting me down. I invite him to shut up."

"That's understandable," I said, "but is it wise? Isn't it possible that by shutting him up you're just bottling up all his fears or worries inside of him? Mightn't it be smarter to encourage him to talk, to verbalize all his frustrations, get them out of his system? Maybe one reason he's full of gloom is that he can never really get rid of it, never truly unburden himself. Maybe you need to learn to absorb some of it for him, as if you were made of emotional blotting paper. That's what I do when my husband gets discouraged. I urge him to talk it out. Believe me, it shortens the period of depression enormously."

"Well," she said, "that makes a lot of sense. But he gets me so upset. I answer him back and before you know it I'm mad and he's mad and it's terrible."

"That isn't being 'emotional blotting paper.' You really have to learn to absorb what is on his mind as he talks it out. Maybe you need some techniques in order to do this."

"Like what?" she asked.

"Oh, there are many. For instance, listen, but don't listen—let it go in one ear and out the other and above all, don't react emotionally to it. Or count to ten. Or look at your husband and think how much you love him. Don't say that aloud. It isn't the right moment. Just think it. And keep thinking of yourself as blotting paper."

"That sure is a new idea," she said thoughtfully. "Do you really do it?"

"Yes," I said, "and you can too."

"Is there anything else?" She had fully convinced me that she wanted help.

"Since you ask," I said with a smile, "I'll suggest a few other things. First, stop thinking of yourself as 'only a wife.' You can influence your husband more than any other person in the world. Make up your mind that you're going to help him with this problem, instead of just enduring it.

"Now what, specifically, can a woman with a gloomy husband do? She can try to change his state of mind by changing what goes into his mind. If he were suffering from a vitamin deficiency, you'd change his diet, wouldn't you? Well, you can change his mental diet, too.

"I've noticed that people who are depressed or gloomy seem to enjoy reading or hearing gloomy things. Try to counteract this tendency. If you take the gloom-peddlers at face value nowadays you'd think that the country has failed, society has failed, the church has failed, everything is going to the dogs. But that's just not so. Point out to your husband that it isn't so. Do a lot of upbeat reading yourself so you always have a story to tell that counteracts this kind of news-distortion.

"Next, look for every exciting, hopeful, optimisitic item you can find in your daily life and pass it on to your husband. If a preacher says something that gives you a lift, hurry home and tell him what it was. Better still, next Sunday ask him to go with you to hear that preacher! If you come across a story that reflects the innate courage or kindness or determination in people, make sure that your husband knows about it too. Feed upbeat things into your conversation with him. Deep down, he must be hungry for this sort of encouragement. In fact, he must be starved for it!"

"I'm sure he is, poor man," she murmured.

"Most people are," I told her. "Twenty-five years ago my husband and I and a friend of ours named Raymond Thornburg started a magazine called *Guideposts.* It has had tremendous success precisely because it fills every issue with true stories of this kind, stories of people who overcome obstacles, who find strength and joy in helping others, who have learned to live positively and happily, who don't let handicaps hold them back or get them down. It's exciting and inspirational and really upbeat all the way. It helps millions of people. It might help your husband too."

"Tell me how I can get it," she said. [Write *Guideposts* Magazine,

Carmel, New York 10512.] "And there's another thing I'm going to do, too. I'm going to try to steer my husband away from people who are downbeat and pessimistic and negative. I'm going to invite positive, clear-thinking people to our home. I can see now that my husband's attitude has attracted a whole lot of pessimists and I'm going to steer him away from them. I can do it and I will!"

"There are a couple of simple exercises," I said, "that you might try—or persuade your husband to try. Just for fun, take a paper and pencil and write down all the good things you can think of about your life together. Or the place where you live. Or a friend that you both know and like. The human mind can't hold two sets of ideas simultaneously. If you make yourself focus on something good, you can't at the same time dwell on something bad.

"And here's another discipline. For one whole day, try to avoid saying anything critical or derogatory about anybody. You may think something negative about somebody, but don't put it into words. This is harder to do than you might suppose. But if you slip on Monday, try again on Tuesday. Keep trying until you've done it for a whole day. Then do it again. I have a friend who gives up saying derogatory things for Lent. She says that at first she finds it terribly difficult. But after trying conscientiously for forty days, she then finds it almost impossible to say anything negative about anybody."

"Why," said my seat companion, "that's a great idea. But for my husband it may be impossible."

"Not if you, yourself, do some of the things we've been talking about," I said. "Not if you really help him."

She laughed. "Not if I do my job as a wife, is that what you mean?"

"That's what I mean," I said.

The seat-belt light had flashed; the plane was beginning its descent into O'Hare airport in Chicago. "You know," my friend said, "it's amazing, really. I mean, hearing your husband preach last Sunday, and then meeting you like this. It's almost as if Somebody or Something planned it this way."

"Who knows?" I said. "Maybe everything that happens is part of a plan."

"It's up to me now," she said. "I know that. Oh, if I can just get some of this across to my husband!"

"You can," I told her. "There's no reason in the world why you and your husband can't become cheerful, optimistic, outgoing people again. Start thinking that and believing it. Act cheerful and optimistic yourself. Forget about the past with its problems and failures. Live in the present. Make the best possible out of today. Ask God to help and guide you. He will. And since He does, what is there to be gloomy about?"

The big plane settled to the ground with hardly a jolt. Neither of us spoke as we taxied up to the unloading ramp. When the plane finally stopped, my companion drew a long breath. "Thanks," she said. "Thanks for everything. You've set me to thinking. What you have suggested won't be easy, but I really feel excited about trying it. Life can change for both of us. It can be an adventure."

"Good luck," I said, and watched her as she made her way up the aisle and out of sight.

EMOTIONS

Sarah Fraser

Living With Depression—and Winning

Sarah Fraser writes about emotional illness with an authority born of experience, describing candidly her own struggle through devastating depression to healing hope. Sarah, familiar with the search by thousands of homemakers for balance, speaks a heart-to-heart language any lay person can understand, clarifying sound scientific "patterns" and Christ's answers for wholeness.

The Cardinal

One day I discovered within myself an utter inability to cope with reality. I had a longing for numbness and even for complete unconsciousness. I opened the door to the medicine cabinet, then shut it resolutely. Suicide was no solution to the problems that were overwhelming me. Yet it seemed there must be some course open that possessed Christian dignity and held some hope of ultimate release.

A dark voice whispered to me, "My dear, there isn't a soul who would blame you. Why, they would rush to your defense. You are hardly responsible for your actions. Think of what you have been going through. Wouldn't you like to wake up in heaven with no more woes, no more ghastly days and nights to face?"

I clutched the fixture before me to keep from swaying. A fresh wave of weakness broke over me. I moved into the bedroom and flung myself across the bed, crying out, "Oh, God, help me!"

When I awakened from sleep I arose, walked past the mirror and shuddered. Even as I looked, the features crumpled into tears. Passing into the kitchen and surveying it, I felt a fresh qualm of responsibility. There were dishes in the sink. If I were gone, who would wash them?

What of my continuing role as a lay worker and a confidante of women in trouble? What of those outside the church who were always so quick to tear Christians to pieces? Turning from the sink, I thought of the words of a chorus:

> Now I belong to Jesus,
> Jesus belongs to me.

But did I? Did he?

I had always enjoyed creative cooking, but now I found it oppressive to prepare and serve even the simplest edible food. My seasonings were "off"; things burned. I kept trying, but everything was a supreme effort.

Wearily I shifted a pile of unmended clothing from a kitchen chair. As I sat down, I lifted the familiar, black-covered Bible from among the tea and coffee cups on the table. Almost indifferently I leafed through First Corinthians until my eye caught a verse in the tenth chapter:

> There hath no temptation taken you but such as is common to . . . women!

Was it a gloss on the text or just my imagination? For the thousandth time I asked, "Is there no spiritual answer to this bottomless depression? Is it really all glands and chemistry and the merry-go-round of the pills?"

My fingers lifted the pages back to the Psalms:

> Thy word have I hid in mine heart, that I might not sin against thee.
>
> Psalms 119:11

That was it. This illness was a sin against God. It involved something deeper than the destruction of health and the interruption of normal family life. I stood at enmity with the Almighty. These frail arms were pushing away the whole universe, yet I was so desperately lonely! And when I went to church, the words of the preachers clattered on my broken spirit as rain falling on a tin roof.

I knew my outlook was being warped by illness, but could not shake the feeling that all life and endeavor were futile. Though I tried hard to "stand on the promises," to recall my interest in the cultural arts, to think of others, I felt stifled by recurring despair. I who had been accused in the past of being voluble now found forming the simplest sentence a struggle. It seemed to me that the power of evil was effectively putting a halt to my prayer life. I, who have often led in public prayer, now could barely formulate the whisper, "Lord, I believe; help thou mine unbelief" (Mark 9:24).

Oh, I knew the words of the Christian message, but what had happened to the music? Was this depression of the devil? Was it true that at one time I had committed my way unto the Lord, and acknowledged him so that he could direct my paths? If that were true, where was he?

It was at this point in my introspection that I looked out the kitchen window and saw a cardinal and its mate perched on a lilac bush. I could not believe it; all we had seen for weeks past were starlings and crows. I reveled in the gorgeous scarlet coloring of the male, the soft hues of the female. The male sang his clear, strong call. Here was a joyful and lovely bit of nature, something cheerful to relate to the family at dinner. Then the pair flew off, and that was all—or so it seemed. I realize now that slight flash of living color was God's harbinger with a special message of hope for me.

Next day I received a letter from my old doctor friend, who had first diagnosed my difficulty. She wrote, "Perhaps the most important reaction I have to your problem is that you do seem to be responding to your own conflicts much as most people do. If when this reaches you, you feel calmer and are able to get some perspective, then you may know what you really want to do to improve the whole pattern. Any thoughtful person may have doubts about his own faith, and certainly about that of others, so your 'rebellion' about this is not foolish, only natural. Perhaps if you decide you've done your best, you can smile and be peaceful and be able to live with yourself. From my view, this is where we all start."

The question was, how did I set about "improving the whole pattern"? Painstakingly I tried to rebuild, to follow the wise advice, and to learn to live above my feelings. With no little trepidation I drew up the following ambitious outline:

1. Take all medication prescribed by the doctor, whether or not it seems to be helping.
2. Try to start, and if possible, to finish some extra household task each day that I don't want to do.

3. Improve body tone by exercising whether or not I want to get off the couch.
4. Answer some of the piled-up correspondence, positively and cheerfully, not seeking sympathy for my plight.
5. Go back to the Sunday School advice: "God first, others second, myself last."
6. Do *something* for the Lord, no matter how weak I feel spiritually and physically. (How often I had advised others to flex their spiritual muscles if they would avoid atrophy, to put their talent to work and not to bury it.)
7. Stifle hurt feelings and animosity at home, regardless of provocation; be as sweet to the family as to outsiders!
8. Resume daily devotions, praying for guidance and joy; exchanging feelings for facts, especially in the worry department. Know and practice replacing the stored depressions with the stored promises of Scripture in my subconscious mind.
9. Put myself in God's pathway, not chiding myself when attention wanders, but giving him the glory when it doesn't. Use my limited strength not selfishly, but for others.

The last rule was the hardest. I hadn't been able to endure myself, far less love myself, so how could I obey God's injunction? Obviously he wanted me to regard myself with respect.

The first step back toward Christian normality came when a neighbor was suddenly taken ill. I was able to help her in conversation and prayer.

Soon afterward I heard an unusual testimony from an outstanding artist. He was a Christian who had turned away from the Lord. One Sunday he stopped in a small church in France where he had sung the year before. An American serviceman was singing the same hymn he had once sung, and was doing it badly. The singer realized that God had taken a weak vessel and had blessed it to his use, that what counts in God's sight is not so much ability as availability. I prayed to make myself available and to have God's message on my lips and in my life.

Soon after that I was asked to speak to a church group. My old fluency had deserted me; how could I address them? I reviewed my personal "Bill of Rights." Yes, I must pay my "do's"! And the verse came: "I can do all things through Christ which strengtheneth me" (Philippians 4:13).

Perhaps you can see now why I have become an avid cardinal-watcher! I am absolutely convinced that God sent that little bit of red into my life to tell me that depression was not his plan for me. He had something better in mind, and he was going to bring it to pass. Odd, isn't it, how a tiny symbol like a cardinal can be used of God to capture the imagination and help to heal the hurts of past and present, and (since we are mortals) probably of future struggles.

Word of my fondness for cardinals seems to have filtered through to some of my friends, who have grasped the deeper significance of the name. One dear friend told me recently that the word *cardinal* comes from the Latin *cardo* which means "a hinge or turning point." Think of it! And the dictionary says there is a related Greek word which means "the waving branch of a tree"! Today the adjective *cardinal* appears to mean something of basic and preeminent importance. To which I can add, "and how!"

During the winter while I wait for spring to come, bringing my little feathered friend in person, I thank God for good furnace heat. I glance around with a smile at the perky cardinal plate on the wall in our front room, and the stained-glass cardinals flying toward each other in our family room windows.

I put on the teakettle, then heat the pot for delicious brew, British fashion, except that mine is about a third as strong. Then I pour the fragrant, steaming tea into my cardinal mug. Refreshed, I step to my small antique desk and prepare to visit with a friend on the West Coast via some cardinal notepaper.

I never tell my husband when I am better. I don't need to. He knows. Even our pets know. Today as I write, I realize it has been a long time since I was cruelly depressed. I sit quietly, collecting my thoughts, realizing that something has happened at last to the dreadful cycle of a few weeks "up" and a few weeks "down."

Yes, I still sag, but only briefly, mildly, and without suicidal desperation. I know that people are praying for me, and I murmur several times a day, "Thank you, Jesus." The vital processes slow down; my head doesn't seem to "work right"; but rather than feel sad, I just feel inefficient. For a few nights there is heavy slumber, and then, praise God, "the fairies come." Six weeks pass without a slump, and I know the hangman's noose has loosened. Life becomes a great, swelling doxology.

Last Christmas I was able to discover anew the truth of Paul's testimony to the power of the living Christ. An opportunity came to join a group that was visiting hospitals. At the time I was feeling weak, but my husband said, "I think you'll feel worse if you don't go." So I went back to the familiar haunts, and found it a victorious experience. As I gave of myself I was blessed in return.

Recently in Catherine Marshall's book *Beyond Our Selves* I reread the chapter "The Prayer of Relinquishment," and discovered afresh the difference between resignation, which is negative, and acceptance, which is positive. I altered my attitude toward my own condition, applying the principle set forth by the author: "Acceptance leaves the door of hope wide open to God's creative plan." I began—oh, so timidly— to thank God for the illness that was bringing me closer to him.

It has been several years since I grappled with myself before the medicine cabinet. Our two sons have grown up and gone, but with maturity has come understanding and love. A car door opens and shuts—my husband is home early from the office. As I stop to give my hair a final pat and add a trace of his favorite cologne, I note that my face is wearing a carefree expression in what I had once thought of as "the dark mirror." Am I "high"? Am I "low"? I know I am not out of the woods by a long way. But I go to the door with a smile of expectancy on my lips, arms outstretched to embrace him. Over his shoulder I see high in the oak tree a cardinal's nest, and I think, "Thank you, Lord, for the blessing of hope."

I Am in a Wilderness Today, God

a wilderness of indecision,
a wilderness of self-doubting,
a wilderness of depression
    of worm-eaten apples,
    of trees that do not bear,
    of rivers with dry beds,
of vines that curl
in the sun, and wither,
    but, Lord, I know
    You know this wilderness
    and every temptation
    to turn back, to cry out, to run,
    to shed your Heavenly mission
and I claim Your victory—
not mine beat out
by limp fledgling wings,
but Yours, the Creator
and Owner of the Universe.

WILMA BURTON

Joyce Landorf

Mourning Song

Joyce Landorf is a woman of many talents—wife, mother, speaker, vocalist, author. Known coast to coast since the publication of her best-seller *The Richest Lady in Town,* her most recent book is a biblical novel *I Came to Love You Late.*

In *Mourning Song* she shares with moving candor the painful lessons death has recently taught her, freeing her to sing of eternal life beginning here and now.

The Lasting Song of Restoration

. . . out of His infinite riches in Jesus
He giveth and giveth and giveth again.

ANNIE JOHNSON FLINT

The work of restoration must happen in our lives after death has taken a loved one away or we may never recover from our loss. We may never pick up the pieces or ever feel whole again.

It is no wonder then, at so many funerals, we hear the Twenty-Third Psalm. If it's not repeated by the minister, rabbi, or priest, it is printed for us to read or its message is brought to us in song, but somehow we are made aware of the poetic beauty of this oft-quoted psalm. Its lyrical prose seems to transcend all racial boundaries and all religious creeds and it is powerful even when the deceased is *not* a Christian.

The reason for its enormous popularity down through the years is its fantastic success in helping to restore our splintered, fractured emotions.

To me the key word is found early in the psalm in the third verse. Here are some translations:

"He restoreth my soul."

"He revives my soul" (MLB).

"He restores my failing health" (LB).

"He restores my soul" (RSV).

All that third verse says basically is:

1. God
2. Heals
3. Me

and it turns out to be the most important message of our life. There we are: alone, sometimes cut in half, weary, and heartsick, when we hear the music of restoration start up with the lyrics:

"Because the Lord is my Shepherd, I have everything I need!"

"He lets me rest in the meadow grass and leads me beside the quiet streams—"

Later, we hear:

"Even when walking through the dark valley of death I will not be afraid, for you are close beside me, guarding, guiding all the way."

As a Christian, God's ability to bring the lasting, continuous song of restoration to my being is just one of the exciting fringe benefits of really knowing Christ.

But what of those who do not know Christ? What good do the magnificent words of the Twenty-Third Psalm do except to pour a little oil on a large, gaping, bleeding wound? What about those bereaved souls who can only guess there *may* be a life after death—or those who "hope" the person who died has gone to a heaven (if there is one)?

I remember the first time I observed people with no hope at a funeral. They had no chance of restoration's song restoring their lives.

They had stumbled into the service on time, but in an alcoholic stupor. I reacted to their being very drunk in a superspiritual (absolutely nauseating) way. "How dare they?" I wondered. Angrily, I silently denounced their actions as definitely in bad taste.

With one destructive blow to my superspiritual pride, God's words cut and leveled me off right at my ankles.

Joyce, why are you so filled with righteous indignation? Why are you so quick to criticize their behavior? Don't you realize they are sorrowing with no *hope? They do not know Me, they do not know I've come to give eternal life, they do not know that there is* more *and they think this is all there is. You must not be angry with them because they have escaped death's ugly reality by drinking. What else do they have to turn to?*

I looked again, this time with a softened heart, at the rather drunk, grieving family of the man in the casket. Even though my compassion was newly acquired, I could clearly see that people without faith, without forgiveness, and without God's peace come to funerals to say good-bye. They do not come to whisper, "I'll see you in the morning." Death comes to them as the finale, the last farewell, the killing blow; and certainly no psalm, even the twenty-third, is going to put things right again. It is easier for them to bear the funeral if their senses are not exposed to the raw, naked hurt of death, so they come in an attitude of numb denial—hardly seeing, hearing, or feeling.

What a difference for the person who comes to Christ, asks Him to forgive his sins, and invites the Lord God into his total life! Living not only completely changes, but so does—*forever*—death and dying! It's a new ball game altogether for Christians. We are not left hopeless, we are not left with *only* these brief days on earth, but, fantastically, we have gained eternity. We do not have to vaguely fantasize about the possibility of reincarnation, or whether or not there *is* life after death—we *know* the positive answers to death's past and future. So when we do sorrow it is this hope of God that will not let us sorrow in terms of *finality* and *defeat*. We are not abandoned to the lonely struggle of living out our frustrating grief alone. In short, our hope in Christ and living after death with Him *is* our restoration.

Paul never said it better and he never said it clearer than when he wrote to the church at Thessalonica:

> And now, dear brothers, I want you to know what happens to a Christian when he dies so that when it happens, you will not be full of sorrow, as those are who have no hope. For since we believe that Jesus died and then came back to life again, we can also believe that when Jesus returns, God will bring back with him all the Christians who have died.
>
> 1 Thessalonians 4:13, 14 LB

As nearly as I can put it together, God does His remarkable work of restoration by three methods . . . . It is my hope—no, my prayer—that God will open your mind, your emotions, and your will to receive *His* restoration. The last thing in the world I want to do is smugly pat you on the back and tell you "everything is coming up roses" or parrot the phrase, "Isn't it nice they (the dead) are with the Lord?" I do not want to be sticky-sweet with a bunch of clichés, pat answers, or unreal phrases. But *God does restore our souls and we can recuperate* from our devastating losses if we are wise enough to hear the inspiring melody of God's mourning song.

Listen, then, to the first faint strains of restoration's song as it begins with one word.

1. *Forgiveness!*

Nothing can be done for us in our grief—whether we are grieving for ourself and our own impending death or for someone else's death—unless we begin with forgiveness.

For the Christian involved in death or dying, forgiveness starts with forgiving (of all people) God! . . .

I spoke at a luncheon this week and a woman heard my brief remarks about this book as I shared some of the lessons I'd learned about death. At the close of the luncheon, while she did not know I'd be writing about forgiveness, she felt led of God to share a personal word or two with me. I'm grateful because she told me of losing her darling, beloved grandson and of her inner reactions that followed. She said there was no way she could accept the little boy's death. She felt angry toward God and could not come up with any reasonable explanation as to why this child had died. The more she thought about it, the madder she got; and one day, as loud and clear as a human voice would sound, she heard the Lord say, *Will you forgive Me for his death?* She said her first reaction was to be stunned by the news that God was *asking* her for forgiveness. Next she realized she had been accusing and blaming God for the death. As soon as she answered the Lord's question with a yes, the peace of God gently slipped into the vacant spot of her heart and she was healed . . . .

Besides forgiving God, we need to forgive ourselves, too. Very often in the days of grief following the loss of a loved one we pile up a huge stack of regrets. We remember each and every thing we did (or did not do) with the deceased and we relive old conflicts. We reconstruct everything we wish we had done and suffer deeply with those regrets and remorseful feelings.

Martha Snell Nicholson said it best when she wrote this poem:

Remembered Sin

I made a lash of my remembered sins.
I wove it firm and strong, with cruel tip,
And though my quivering flesh shrank from the scourge,
With steady arm I plied the ruthless whip.

For surely I, who had betrayed my Lord,
Must needs endure this sting of memory.
But though my stripes grew sore, there came no peace,
And so I looked again to Calvary.

His tender eyes beneath the crown of thorns
Met mine; His sweet voice said, "My child, although
Those oft-remembered sins of thine have been
Like crimson, scarlet, they are now like snow.

"My blood, shed here, has washed them all away,
And there remaineth not the least dark spot,
Nor any memory of them; and so
Should you remember sins which God forgot?"

I stood there trembling, bathed in light, though scarce
My tired heart dared to hope. His voice went on:
"Look at thy feet, My child." I looked, and lo,
The whip of my remembered sins was gone!

I'm sure God longs to take away our whips of remembered sins. But if those painful slashes on our souls are ever to heal, we need to forgive ourselves as God has forgiven us. We need to deliberately dwell on the important fact that when God *forgave* those sins and past regrets He *forgot* them as well.

After we have checked out our forgiveness and seen if it's updated to forgive God and self, then we may need to see if forgiveness is needed toward other people.

The healing that follows forgiveness in my own case came after I forgave God for the death of our son and then forgave (by God) my parents for their not attending David's funeral. Until I put my regrets and angers into God's hands I was sick, not only physically, but emotionally as well.

When we can lay the people, places, and events into the forgiving hands of God, we have taken a major step toward healthy, normal living once more. In fact, there is nothing we can do with the regretful people and events of yesterday except entrust them to the God of all tomorrows.

If the first strains of God's song of restoration begin with forgiveness, then you can rest assured the bridge part of the melody in the middle of the song will be acceptance.

2. *Acceptance.*

In learning about dying and transferring the lessons on to me, my mother lived the best, most profound moments of all her life. I will remember her for many years of delightful things, but I will remember her most for her *attitude* of acceptance toward her own death during her last seven weeks.

I pray I will be able to teach the God-given attitudes of acceptance to my children even before it is time for me to keep my appointment with death. I have been working on it now for several years.

Fear and denial are at the opposite ends of the world from acceptance and I must realize this when I begin to teach my children about death and dying. I wish I had started out earlier with our children, but like every other parent in the world, I felt our children would know soon enough about death's dark curtain and I thought, "Why bring it up?"

But death is a vital part of living and preparation and discussion of this almost taboo subject will be valuable to them as they mature into adults.

Children should be included in before- and after-death conversation and they should be allowed to hear the funeral plans and decisions being made. It's not a time to hustle them outside or stop talking about "Grandma who just died" when they enter a room. To let them listen to our grief and see our tears is to let them know *their* grief is not abnormal. They are feeling sad, too, and to include them in our discussions and to answer their questions helps them to allow the work of mourning to be accomplished.

Recently on a TV special called "The Right to Die," Dr. Elisabeth Kübler-Ross stated that she felt children must be able to accept death and its processes at least by the time they are twenty years of age. She went on to state that if they had not come to grips with death acceptance by their twenties then it would be very hard on them later when they tried to cope with death.

A couple of years ago our family had quite a discussion about accepting death. We talked about the "what ifs" of dying.

What if Dad died?

What if Mom died?

What if you died? What would you want for your funeral?

And the conversation which started during dinner went on long after dinner was finished.

We will always remember the discussion. The reasons none of us will ever forget that night are twofold: (1) For some strange reason, we all waxed hysterically funny in the wit department, and (2) we made some serious statements that will be remembered and (some of them) carried out in the event of our deaths . . . .

While we laughed and loved a great deal that night, we took some serious steps toward firming up acceptance of death as a part of living in all our hearts—not just our children's. We concluded that really the funeral should be a *Christian worship service to God in loving memory of the one who had died.*

Not only must we teach our children acceptance of the death process, but we must work with acceptance on our own part. Nothing facilitates this faster than making out a will.

Frankly, I never did think too much about our making out a will. I felt my husband and I (in our forties) were too young to bother with it, and to procrastinate seemed to be the best plan. Also, since I'll probably do my best to spend most of what is allotted to us financially in life, I really didn't think there would be too much left after we died to divide and conquer.

That was before I read a powerful message in Catherine Marshall's *To Live Again,* which was, "Peter . . . had left no will."

It was in those few printed pages that Catherine Marshall related the horror and agony she endured after her husband died, leaving no will. After reading it, my husband and I came to a point of decision: we would make out a will immediately. So we did!

Our education on what happens to "property and things" after death escalated considerably. We found that if, at the time of death, there is no written, valid will, the *state chooses* the beneficiaries of all *your* properties and the state's decisions are absolutely final!

We also found that many, many Christians (something like eight out of ten) do not write any will at all. Out of the few Christians who do make wills, almost 50 percent do *not* remember the Lord's work or their home church.

Some of the bereaved I've talked with have been stumbling down dark, discouraging corridors for years because no will was left. Any money they thought they had was used up in probate taxes, and went to state funds. Having no will produced one financial headache after another for them. Acceptance of death is next to impossible with these overwhelmingly disturbing financial burdens. To experience the agonies of settling an estate (even a very small one) is to experience frustrations of the greatest magnitude.

Should the day come when our children must decide what to do with our possessions, they will have a clear, concise, valid will to direct them. Also, we have left for them a Christian will—one which provides for them *and* the Lord's work.

After our children are taken care of, our will leaves a percentage of our "estate" to our church and to a couple of marvelous Christian organizations. That is one way to do it (by percentages); but our friend and business executive, Roark Moudy, has his will bequeathing cash monies to the Lord's work, and either way is fine!

The actual financial amount of our estate is not too fantastic, but the peace of mind for our children and the knowledge that our money will go to the Lord's work (and not someone else's) pushes us out of denial into healthy acceptance.

We encourage acceptance not only by freely discussing death and dying with our families and by making sure there is a valid will, but by one other important way as well: by understanding the five stages of death and dying.

Remember? Denial, anger, bargaining, depression, and finally, acceptance. The dying go through these stages and so do those standing by. The time of bereavement will probably produce them again and you may feel like your life is a rerun of some oft-seen TV program. Don't be impatient or discouraged, just remember the ultimate goal of these stages is to get to acceptance.

Karen was a gal who had worked her way through those stages to acceptance. Six months before she died, she said to one of our pastors, "Keith, whatever time I have left, I'm not going to leave sad, grief-stricken memories. But by the grace of God, I'm going to leave happy, victorious times and memories for my family." And so she *did!* But, like her family and those of us who are left behind, we must remember those difficult stages may appear many months after we think we are "over" our grief . . . .

If the first part of God's restoration song begins with forgiveness, and then moves into the melody of acceptance, it is the incredible finale of hope that brings me up out of my seat to applaud and shout, "Bravo!"

3. *Hope.*

God gives hope in several ways, but one of the best is with the poetry He has written through others.

As I look back now, I can see that just before I experienced the deaths of my son, grandfather, and mother, God was tuning up His orchestra for the song of hope.

Only a bare two months before David died, a friend of mine introduced me to the writings of Martha Snell Nicholson. What seemed then like a casual remark by Al Sanders—"Joyce, you'll love her poems," turned out to be far more succinct than imagined.

I can see in retrospect that God deliberately turned my heart to her writings. What made her poems special was that she wrote all of them while confined to her bed as an invalid . . . .

During the dark months of blindly stumbling around, trying to heal physically from the surgery and emotionally from David's death, I received hundreds of letters which included poems . . . . Then, when my mother died, I received this letter from my millionaire friend, Mary Korstjens.

Dearest Joyce,

You and your family are on my mind and heart so much these days.

The book of poems by Martha Snell Nicholson that you lent me once, had the two poems I have enclosed. They were very precious to me when my mom went to be with God.

Joyce, may God's love sustain and strengthen you beyond belief.

All my love and prayers,
MARY

One of those poems . . . became my theme song over the next years. I still never read it without thinking of the pain-racked, bedridden little lady who stubbornly refused to give in to her own agony and penned:

The Heart Held High

God made me a gift of laughter
And a heart held high,
Knowing what life would bring me
By and by,

Seeing my roses wither
One by one,
Hearing my life-song falter,
Scarce begun,

Watching me walk with Sorrow. . . .
That is why
He made me this gift of laughter—
This heart held high!

MARTHA SNELL NICHOLSON

Martha Snell Nicholson also helped me in my concept of what death is really all about by this poem:

The Other Side

This isn't death—it's glory!
It is not dark—it's light!
It isn't stumbling, groping,
Or even faith—it's sight!
This isn't grief—it's having
My last tear wiped away;
It's sunrise—it's the morning
Of my eternal day!

This isn't even praying—
It's speaking face to face;
Listening and glimpsing
The wonders of His grace.
This is the end of pleading
For strength to bear my pain;
Not even pain's dark mem'ry
Will ever live again.

How did I bear the earth-life
Before I came up higher,
Before my soul was granted
Its ev'ry deep desire,
Before I knew this rapture
Of meeting face to face
The One who sought me, saved me,
And kept me by His grace!

By her writings, I found Mrs. Nicholson did not live in denial, anger, bargaining, or depression, but in a hope-filled acceptance of life *and* dying . . . .

Our hearts are mended by poetry, especially the honest, valid work borne out of heartaches and matured by God's direction.

Our souls are also healed by prose writings and songs.

God used Dr. Elisabeth Kübler-Ross's book as well as His Own Word, and eventually He led me to books (sometimes just a paragraph or two) which spoke directly and decisively to my needs.

The strongest writing, filled with the most hope, I found was God's Word.

To His friend, Martha, Jesus laid on the line our unconquerable position as Christians on hope and life after death when He said:

> I am the one who raises the dead and gives them life again. Anyone who believes in me, even though he dies like anyone else, shall live again.
>
> John 11:25 LB

These powerful words transform "I *guess* so," and "I *hope* so," and "I *wish* so," into "I KNOW SO!"

The vigor and the vitality of Jesus' words fill in the missing parts in the musical arrangement of my mourning song. John picks up the refrain for me whenever I read his words:

> And what is it that God has said? That he has given us eternal life, and that this life is in his Son. So whoever has God's Son has life; whoever does not have his Son, does not have life.
>
> 1 John 5:11, 12 LB

So, if you are a Christian (one who has believed on the Lord Jesus Christ; who has asked for forgiveness of sins) then you have been *guaranteed* life—not just here, but forever. This hope separates the men from the boys, the women from the girls; so we, who have Christ, can look death, dying, and sorrow right on, eyeball-to-eyeball, and not flinch. Death is ugly and it is repulsive, but it is *not,* I repeat, *not* able to bring the life of a Christian to a dreadful, screeching halt. God has worked out an alternate plan and it is a plan filled with soaring hope . . . .

It is this hope of heaven, this shining promise of life after death, that restores our confidence. The lovely confidence I saw in my mother while she was dying began to grow in *my* heart after she died, once I realized what a wealth of restoration was in the Christian's hope . . . .

The early Christians heard the mourning song of God and as they were being led to their horrendous deaths in the Roman arena, they picked up mourning song's tune and we are told "went to their death—*singing.*" It is not possible to be scared to death and still sing. The vocal cords restrict themselves into hard, rigid, tautly pulled ropes that will not work. So those martyred Christians had to have the song of God's confidence and joy really bursting within them in order to have filled the Coliseum with the sound of their music.

When I read, "Tears of joy shall stream down their faces, and I will lead them home with great care" (Jeremiah 31:9 LB), I can, in my mind's eye, see not only those early Christians, but all the precious children of God we have lost; and, as if they are being filmed for a great movie spectacular, they stand together, all on a supersized screen. They stand as a gigantic host of people in front of me and the stereophonic music pours out of hundreds of speakers over my soul. Beautifully, as I listen and watch, I see God leading them *home*—with "great care."

Over the visual picture and above the sound of the triumphant music, I hear the narrator. He reads from a script written by Jeremiah and his resonant words ring deep and clear:

> They shall come home and sing songs of joy upon the hills of Zion, and shall be radiant over the goodness of the Lord . . . . Their life shall be like a watered garden, and all their sorrows shall be gone.
>
> Jeremiah 31:12 LB

They are not the only ones who can sing the songs of Zion—we who are left can sing, too. We are not suffering from frozen vocal cords that are stiff because of fear, absent because of denial, or tight because of anger and bitterness that would give us laryngitis.

Forgiveness, acceptance, and hope have warmed and toned up the flexibility of the vocal cords; and so with full, strong, healthy voices we can sing the songs of restoration and hope!

We can sing the old hymns of the church like Fanny Crosby's "Blessed Assurance," or Spafford's and Bliss's "It Is Well With My Soul," or the song J. A. Crutchfield wrote called "Zion's Hill," with the very boldness and confidence of God.

We can sing the newer songs of restoration like Bill Gaither's "He Touched Me," Audrey Mieir's "Don't Spare Me," or Ruth Calkin's "But I Do Know" with God's authority giving a positive, honest reality to our vocal tones.

And we can sing songs like this one:

He Giveth More

He giveth more grace when the burdens grow greater,
He sendeth more strength when the labors increase;
To added affliction He addeth His mercy,
To multiplied trials, His multiplied peace.

When we have exhausted our store of endurance,
When our strength has failed ere the day is half done,
When we reach the end of our hoarded resources,
Our Father's full giving is only begun.

His love has no limit, His grace has no measure,
His power no boundary known unto men;
For out of His infinite riches in Jesus
He giveth and giveth and giveth again.

ANNIE JOHNSON FLINT

We can sing because we *know* Hope and we *experience* Hope daily! Because of Hope's song, we can move, work, and make our time here really count . . . .

So I have listened and heard this remarkable song. The hope of the music creeps over the hills and valleys of my life and heals, warms, and motivates me to action. I *can* carry on, I *can* last, I can even *sing* because of the aliveness of God in my soul.

The sound of God's powerful lasting song of restoration has begun with the opening theme of forgiveness; and finally it arrives at the chorus and final *coda* with hope, glorious hope, *crescendo*ing up around us in fully orchestrated, stereophonic sound!

It is as we *allow* our ears to hear this concluding section of music that God reveals the full-blown beauty of His tender, moving mourning song.

It is also this part, the hope part of the song, which lingers in our minds. Long after the song has ended, even during those dark, forbidding hours just before dawn, we can recall the lyric and melody line of hope; and to our amazement we can sing the heady, glorious song for whatever life-span we have left!

Ethel Waters

To Me It's Wonderful

Ethel Waters, internationally loved artist—singer and actress—captured a vast new audience when she joined the Billy Graham Evangelistic Team to whom she will always be "Mom." While her incomparable way with a gospel song brought thousands to their feet cheering, Ethel Waters's only desire, childlike and reverent, was to glorify her Lord.

I was bitter as well as lonesome for Jesus when I rededicated my life to Him back at the 1957 New York Crusade. And the big reason *then* for my painful bitterness was that I was so *fat.*

I hated my size and I had grown bitter about it. Not so much because I knew I didn't look good anymore—I wasn't bitter because I'd lost my good figure—but because all my life I had been an *active* person with no need to be size conscious. I was always fairly immune to flattery. A handshake if it was sincere meant more than a eulogy.

Of course, seeing that weight begin to pile on, I adored the sweat baths and massages I began to take, but it was then I found out to my horror that I had built up a solid *fat foundation.* I also discovered that fat is like a fungus, you can remove the top layer, but the bottom remains dormant, and is the hardest and last to go.

As the pounds piled on, I found I was having terrible difficulty doing just the ordinary things, and my bitterness grew faster than the fat. I'd try to diet and I'd take those steam baths and massages, but by the time I was in my late fifties, I believed I would just have to endure and learn to adjust to this terrible affliction. Never having had to give a thought to my weight, it sneaked up on me. My bitterness became almost a second handicap. It turned to out-and-out *hatred* when it seemed everybody went out of their way to tell me how fat I was.

I hated and I was bitter. Part of what bugged me was having *closets* (plural) *full of expensive complete outfits* and then ending up at Lane Bryant's to hunt something I could get into. And sometimes even they didn't have my size! The woes of becoming a fat, middle-aged woman with no previous experience at coping with the menace of an unwieldy body are horrible. It seemed to me it had all happened overnight. Of course, it didn't, but learning to live with it was a brand new experience when I reached the place where I was getting in my own way.

Now, I had always been the type of person to face facts, and one day I decided to *force* myself to open one of those well-filled closets, select a dress and try it on. I should have said *try* to try it on, because there I stood in front of a full-length mirror stuck part way into that small-sized dress and what I saw was so *grotesque,* I got to laughing and couldn't stop. That was *before* Billy's Crusade in 1957, but I know the moment of laughter was my heavenly Father's way—with one stroke—of winning that battle. As I stood there laughing, I faced the truth about what had really happened to me and instantly the hatred and bitterness began to drain away. The fat didn't drain away in an instant, let me tell you, but I had my rose-tinted glasses *off* and was seeing myself as I really was: a big fat, middle-aged, gray-haired woman. *Overstuffed.* I also faced what I had been told, that fat doesn't stand still. It is constantly multiplying and this is the Voice of Experience speaking!

I was not a professing Christian then, although I had always talked to God when I was alone, but as I stood there looking so grotesque and laughing so hard at myself, I could feel the warmth of His smile.

Looking at fat, aging Ethel Waters in that full-length mirror, and laughing, my mind went back to when I was a child and laughed and thought certain old folks were funny—what they did, what they wore—especially if they were fat! Back in those days people were themselves and didn't put on so many airs. The children laughed at the old folks' get-ups and certain funny things they did. Still you had to mind and obey them because they were grown-ups. At least you did to their faces, but that didn't stop you from having some pretty ornery thoughts even though you really loved them.

I thought first of old Aunt Betsy, whom I dearly loved, but who was no relation. She lived in a one-room rear house and oh, she was *fat* and she dipped snuff, so she was always drooling. Aunt

Betsy wore about four petticoats, a thick skirt, a blouse, a man's sweater and a starched apron. I loved to be around her when I was seven or eight just to watch the expert way she could aim and never miss when she would *skeet* that snuff. (Meaning to a younger generation that she could spit a great distance and never miss.) Aside from her expert *skeeting*, Aunt Betsy was also a midwife, so one day when she was out delivering a baby, I decided to try to skeet the way she did. I opened her snuffbox and poured some in the lid the way I'd seen her do it, then I pulled down my bottom lip and began to pour it in. I must have had too much in the lid or was shaking too hard, because I ended up with snuff in my mouth, up my nose, my eyes burning, and instead of *skeeting* I was swallowing! I made a B-line for the outhouse and sick as a yellow dog, I begged the Lord to please forgive me and also not to let Aunt Betsy or my own Aunt Vi find out what I'd done!

Still standing in front of that mirror with that small-sized dress on as far as it would go, I thought, "You're a lot like Aunt Betsy! You can skeet (water) through your teeth and you're getting old and your hair is gray—and you're *fat*." . . .

You see, when I was a child, I had no weight problem. Sometimes I didn't have enough to eat, but if we had food, I could eat a ton without giving it a thought. That was true until my late fifties, when I began to inflate like a big old balloon. Even though it didn't all come on as fast as it seemed to me, I was just not in any way accustomed to fat, to the handicap of a cumbersome body. Don't laugh at a fatty. They're *handicapped.* But if they've grown up with fat, at least they know something about how to handle themselves. What to expect. What not to try to do! I didn't. It frightened me. I felt so helpless so much of the time before and for the months after my rededication to Christ, I would cry out to Him, pleading for Him to help me to learn to adjust, just to handle myself in everyday things. It's a miserable feeling to go to somebody's house, sit down in a chair, and the chair breaks! It isn't funny. It's tragic.

I got to the place where I was afraid to sit down, and I was too tired and too big to stand up. I would get on a plane, and the first time that happened, I remember, I didn't know to ask for an extension belt and the seat belt wouldn't go around me and I was panic-stricken! I finally learned from a nice little stewardess that they had extension belts for corpulent people, but once I remember they didn't have one and had to hold the plane while they sent somebody to get one that would go across my fat stomach. Another time, there wasn't an extension belt to be found, so the pilot had to make an easy landing because there I sat without a belt!

I've told you about those early days when my children at the Crusades would so kindly let me come just to be with them and to hear Billy preach. Of course, I was still so terribly big and would be so miserable they would have a doctor available at whatever city I joined them and he would give me medication. Different women members of the Crusades and the wives of the Team boys helped me rest enough so I could sing, or at least sit up long enough to hear my child, Billy, preach. You know I *longed* to be fed spiritually, or in my miserable condition both during the Crusade in New York and in those first months afterward, I would never have made the effort to get there.

I've always been conscious of what I wear, too. I don't think I was a clothes horse, but I didn't like to wear anything that wasn't right and I was then just big all over—but bigger in the stomach! Buying anything to wear was like a bad dream I had to live through. One day I got a bright idea. I'd looked at some pictures of what I thought were smart outfits for large women. Then I realized they were maternity dresses! But they were sharp. So one day I was standing in front of the window of a beautiful shop where they had on display all these dresses for pregnant women. I hadn't gone in yet. I was just standing near the door still looking in the window. I said, "Lord, they sure look good, don't they?" And about that time a saleslady noticed me with my huge stomach and she came to the open door of the shop and said, "If we don't have your size, madame, we can order it."

I looked at her, then I thought to myself, "Nothing but a try beats a failure. I might as well go in there and try!" After all, I knew *mine* was permanent.

And do you know, I got the cutest dress that covered how big my stomach was? I did, and it looked so good, I could wear it to a Crusade and I did! There I was, sashayin' around all dressed up. I've never told this story on myself before, but it's true.

It's true and it's funny.

When I was touring with Cy Jackson and *Music for America* during that same big fat period, they had to work around and find a mike I could hang around my neck because my big stomach kept me too far away from the floor mike. There was *no way* to get the mike close enough to me as it would pick up my voice right. That big stomach took up just too much room for sound transmission. I had decided I'd do fine though if I could just lean into the curve of the piano to sing. I *had* to touch something because I was so ill from that fat around my heart, I never knew when I was going to fall. And if I fell, who could get me up? I stood in the wings too, until it was my time to come on, because I was afraid to sit down. I refused, even when they worried about my getting too tired and running short of breath. I refused. I just said, "Cy, I can't do it!" I'd have been too emotionally upset to sing, so I'd breathe, "Lord, please don't make me have to sit down! Please!"

I did all right singing, leaning there in the curve of the piano, touching it with my hand to steady myself, until at one curtain call, something happened in the line-up of the cast and somebody else got into my curve in that piano for the finale. Bless the Lord, I had to stand out in front! I stood there because there wasn't anyplace else to stand. I couldn't suddenly shift the whole cast around in front of all those people. But when the curtain started down, and they saw it coming and me standing out there in front, they shifted all right! Oh, they started moving fast, because there was just no way—they knew it and I knew it—for that heavy curtain to get past my stomach!

The audience got the message, and to coin a phrase, "It was fantastic!"

Now, I've told some of these funny things about my own fat—for whom it may concern. If you're not fat yet—don't. If you're fat, get it off, or it can kill you. I know.

How did I get it off? Almost 200 pounds? I stayed under my doctor's care and prayed to my heavenly Father to help me. He did . . . .

I was on a big plane once when a man got on who was pretty far gone from drinking. The stewardess hesitated to let him sit beside me, but I didn't. I said to let the poor fellow sit right down. Finally, when he got around to talking to me, I could see he was just all to pieces. Of course, they wouldn't give him another drink even though he wanted one, but he was in bad shape. I could tell he had a terrible problem of some kind. He looked so miserable.

"Why don't you eat something, child?" I asked him.

"I don't wanna eat. I wan' another drink."

I said, "But drinking hasn't solved your problem, why not try some food instead?"

He just looked at me.

"You've been smoking one cigarette after another ever since the plane got off the ground. Soon as one goes out, you light another and that hasn't helped either."

He looked so unhappy, so distressed, but he didn't answer. He just looked at me. I went on, "I don't know what your problem is, but I know you can be helped. I *know* it."

He turned in his seat and asked, "What's your name?"

"My name's Ethel Waters."

"*You*—Ethel Waters?"

"Yes."

"*The* Ethel Waters?"

"*Just* Ethel Waters."

After a few seconds he asked me where I was going, and I told him I was going to a Crusade. Then he told me his name and began to get very serious, like a troubled little boy.

Finally, he said, "There's something about you reminds me of someone very close—a woman who helped raise me. You're just like her."

The poor fellow, whose name I forget, except that his nickname was Red, told me the name of the woman who'd raised him was Tempy. She'd looked after him from the time he was a baby and I reminded him of her, so he began then to tell me about his horrible burden. He was going to bury his daughter, who had been a beautiful musician. She had called him to come to a certain concert she was giving and he didn't go. Now he was heartsick. His lovely daughter had been killed in an automobile accident.

I tried to let him know that I understood and that I cared about him, but he was in no condition for a lot of talk. I then told him I wanted him to eat something and not take one more drink. "After you've had some food to soak up that liquor, I want you to put your head on my shoulder and take a nap. That way you'll be able to face what's up ahead. When you get off this plane, whoever meets you will know you're—a *man*."

He looked at me again and said, "Lord, that's just the way Tempy would have said it!"

When he had sat down, he was loud and boisterous. I understood why he was. He was striking out at life because of his hurt, his hideous pain. That was natural. He had the crew and the other passengers all concerned that he was going to annoy everybody for the whole trip. I sensed that what he needed was comfort. I'd needed comfort myself for so long and never found it until I found Jesus. They brought the food, he ate, and in no time he had dropped his head on my shoulder and he slept like a baby for at least an hour and a half.

My shoulder got a little kinked sitting in one position, but I wouldn't have shifted around for anything. I just sat there and said, "Lord, let this child sleep—let me sleep."

As I recall, we were changing planes in Atlanta. I asked the stewardess for a cold, wet towel and then I woke him up when I saw we were almost there. He wiped his face off good, combed his hair, looked me straight in the eye and said, soberly now, "I *do* want to thank you."

I patted his hand. "Honey, thank the Lord. He knew what you needed right then. Now you go on and get off this plane and meet your aunt or your sister, or whoever, and don't you take another drink. Don't waste your time trying to thank me. You'll need it all. The Lord knew you needed some rest and He found this shoulder. You just needed a shoulder when you got on this plane. And whenever you look to Him, He's always going to let you find a shoulder when you need it. You see, son, there are more Tempys around."

I was glad I hadn't lost too much weight. That boy needed a good shoulder.

RENEWAL

Catherine Marshall

Adventures in Prayer

Catherine Marshall scarcely needs an introduction to the countless readers here and abroad who have made her books inspirational classics. Speaker, consultant, best-selling author, she and her husband, Leonard LeSourd, former editor of *Guideposts,* divide their time between their home on Florida's east coast and Evergreen Farm in Virginia.

The Prayer in Secret

In the summer of 1960—when I saw for the first time the Sistine Chapel in Rome—I was intrigued to learn something of the working habits of Michelangelo Buonarroti. The four years that it took the great Florentine to paint the vault of the chapel were largely spent in isolation behind locked doors. While very young, Michelangelo had found that for him, work of integrity was impossible without secrecy.

Learning this reminded me again of the power that lies in secrecy. It was in connection with my first book, *A Man Called Peter,* that I experienced its validity. After a rough outline had been approved by the publishers, some instinct told me that until the book was completed, the work should be kept as secret as possible.

Looking back now, I can see at least two reasons why this secrecy was right. I knew that the creativity necessary for the writing was a delicate plant indeed. It could easily wither and die under discouragement or nonconstructive criticism.

I also knew that the ideas of others might cloud my own, could dull and confuse those deepest inner convictions that had to be followed for writing integrity.

Many another writer has found that when he shares an idea for an article or a book too soon, his ability to get the idea on paper sharply deteriorates.

Ernest Hemingway, for instance, has described the trouble he plunged himself into while working on the manuscript of *The Sun Also Rises.* The setting was the village of Schruns in the Austrian Alps. Around the fireside of a winter's evening, Hemingway made the mistake of reading aloud portions of his novel. The danger to him was not negative criticism, rather damage to his own critical judgment through too much unthinking praise, as he describes in *A Moveable Feast:*

> When they said, "It's great, Ernest. Truly, it's great," I wagged my tail in pleasure . . . instead of thinking, "If they . . . like it, what is wrong with it?" That was what I would think if I had been functioning as a professional—although if I had been functioning as a professional, I would never had read it to them.

It was after I had discovered the power of secrecy in the arts that I realized its strength in the equally creative realm of prayer.

In the Sermon on the Mount, Jesus reveals the mysterious spiritual power in secrecy: "But when thou doest alms, let not thy left hand know what thy right hand doeth: That thine alms may be in secret: and thy Father which seeth in secret himself shall reward thee openly" (Matthew 6:3, 4).

In addition to charitable giving and good deeds, Jesus applied the principle specifically to two other areas—prayer (Matthew 6:5, 6) and spiritual disciplines such as fasting (Matthew 6:16–18).

One man who took these words literally was George Müller. The result was a story of prayer power that amazed the world. Müller, a German with a practical businessman's mind, was seized with the conviction that he should establish orphanges in nineteenth-century England where there were few provisions for homeless children.

Especially astounding in view of his business background, was the way in which Müller determined to raise the money for this project—by secret prayer. His associates were appalled when he spelled out some of the details:

- No funds would be solicited directly. The method for obtaining contributions would be by prayer *alone.* No worker could give out information about specific needs.
- Names of contributors would also be kept secret. They would

be thanked privately. Nor would prominent names ever be used to advertise the institution.

- In spite of these seemingly unpromising preconditions, no debts were to be incurred—all transactions were strictly cash.

George Müller then set aside one hour each day for prayer. As punctually as a Swiss watch, George would retire to his room at the allotted time. On his knees he could concentrate on meeting his Lord, pouring out to God his wishes and hopes and dreams for his work and the needs of his orphans. Once every week, he met with all his associates in a session of prayer—also behind closed doors.

There was something so irresistibly challenging about Müller's formula that despite his aversion to publicity, the news traveled and purses were eagerly opened. Starting with one rented house, two workers, and forty-three children, in time there were five new buildings and 110 workers for 2,050 orphans. In all, during his lifetime, 121,000 orphans were sheltered, fed, educated—a million and a half pounds sterling administered. (Müller kept careful records of every transaction.) The work is still going on as a monument to faith. And at its heart was the Prayer in Secret.

As we walk with Jesus through the Gospel narratives, we find Him acting on this principle Himself. On one occasion when He had just healed a leper, we are told that "Jesus sent him away . . . with the strict injunction, 'Mind you say nothing at all to anybody' " (Mark 1:43, 44 PHILLIPS). At another time, when Jesus had raised Jairus's twelve-year-old daughter, we read that her restoration sent her parents almost "out of their minds with joy. But Jesus gave them strict instructions not to let anyone know what had happened . . ." (Mark 5:42, 43 PHILLIPS).

The Prayer in Secret need not conflict with praying two-by-two or with small-group prayer. When Jesus raised Jairus's daughter, there were seven persons in the room—the girl, the child's parents, Peter, James, and John, and Christ. Yet following such a group experience, Jesus seems to say that additional power is released if there is no gossip about it outside the prayer room.

When I first read these accounts of Christ's ministry, I assumed that He wanted certain miracles kept secret lest He not be able to cope with the eager crowds or because this might speed Him on His way to the Cross prematurely. But I believe that a more significant reason is involved—that answers to prayer can be diminished, even nullified, by exposing the experience to the comments of the unbelieving. When Jesus returned to His hometown, Nazareth, where the townspeople thought of Him merely as the local carpenter's son, we are told: "And he did not many mighty works there because of their unbelief" (Matthew 13:58).

Since this happened to Christ Himself, then how much more easily it could happen to any of us!

How Jesus loved to pray in secret Himself! He had a habit of "rising up a great while before day" and going outdoors—to a mountainside or some other deserted place—to pray. Perhaps because of the small, crowded Palestinian houses, that was the only way He could find privacy and solitude.

Before major decisions—such as His choosing of the twelve apostles—He would pray alone an entire night. And going back to the beginning of His public ministry, we find Jesus going off into the desert for forty days and forty nights of seclusion and concentrated prayer. He knew that power was needed; in secret He would find it.

There are other reasons why Jesus instructs us to pray in secret. Real power in prayer flows only when man's spirit touches God's Spirit. As in worship, so in prayer: "God is a Spirit: and they that worship him must worship him in spirit and in truth" (John 4:24). Secrecy helps us get rid of hindrances to praying with our spirit. For instance, in our room with the door shut, we are not so likely to strut and pose and pretend as we are when another human being is present. We know that we cannot deceive God. Transparent honesty before Him is easier for us in isolation.

Then too, there is the necessity of shutting out distractions—the doorbell, the telephone, the laundryman, the children. God asks that we worship Him with concentrated minds as well as allowing the Spirit to direct our wills and emotions. A divided and scattered mind is not at its most receptive.

There is also the matter of our spiritual balance sheets. When we perform a good deed, we are usually quick to advertise it, display it, collect the credit—use it up. Unworthy or bad deeds we hide. The "credit" (i.e. debit) of the bad acts stays with us, accumulates. Thus our personalities are always on the debit side. Spiritually we remain chronically bankrupt.

Jesus told us that if we want to become fulfilled and productive persons, we must reverse the process. That is, we are to divest ourselves of weaknesses, faults, and sins by confessing them openly, while kindnesses and good deeds are to be kept secret. The result is an inner reservoir of power.

As the reservoir begins to fill, we experience the Father's "reward" as promised by Jesus: God's presence in our life and affairs with all the attendant blessings.

What these blessings turn out to be can be shared with others only long after our Prayer in Secret has been answered. That is why I can now tell about our prayer for the Stowe family. (Of course, this is not their real name.)

It happened one autumn when our children were small. We knew Mr. Stowe because he was a schoolteacher in our son's school, a man who gave all of himself to his profession. As such, he symbolized to us all those unsung citizens who serve selflessly but often with small pay. The Stowes had five children, lived in a house too small for such a large family, and were having a hard time making it financially. Yet they could always be counted on for community projects. But we knew that they themselves had too few of the necessities and none of those extras of the good life that some of us take for granted.

Our concern took the form of dinner-table conversations followed later on by some prayer for the Stowes during one of our Family Times. Then we asked the question, "Lord, is there anything You would like *us* to do for the Stowes?"

The answer was not long in coming. We were directed back to an old novel we had all but forgotten, Lloyd C. Douglas's *The Magnificent Obsession.* As we refreshed our minds about the story, we remembered that Randolph, a sculptor, found that when he gave money away as Jesus instructed in the Sermon on the Mount, without letting anyone discover his generous action, power flowed into his life through new energy in his work, fresh sureness and poise in relationships with people, and answered prayers. The sculptor's petition was not for money or fame, but rather for his work: ". . . the capacity to do just one credible work of statuary."

Randolph's prayer was abundantly answered—he became a gifted sculptor. Eventually in fact, fame and material benefits followed as well.

In Douglas's book the "secret of keeping a secret" was then passed on to others—including a brain surgeon—with equally startling results.

All of this led to our deciding to make the Stowes' Christmas a family project, and to keep this a secret from the Stowes as from everyone else.

Other ground rules were laid down: We were to make as many of the presents as possible—like cakes and cookies from cherished old recipes, sequined and beribboned Christmas ornaments; a tiny Christmas tree for the birds, decorated with eatable goodies for them. In addition, our children were to save or earn the money for at least one gift for each of the Stowes.

By Christmas Eve a large carton was filled to the brim with gifts. Attached was a note explaining to our friends that these gifts were to try to say to them how much their continual unselfish giving had meant to many in the community; that since this gift was from the Christ Child Himself, other names were not needed. With each gift went a prayer for God's abundant blessing on their family. The box was then left on the Stowes' doorstep.

And the giving and Prayer in Secret was marvelously answered. Word came to us that the Stowes had one of the greatest Christmases of their lives. Not long after that, Mr. Stowe was offered a better position with a larger salary. Suddenly, the whole community began to show more appreciation for the Stowes' selfless service. The children found various ways to go to college. Blessings for all of us came out of the experience.

Because the prime condition of this prayer *is* secrecy, illustrations beyond one's personal experience with it are not easily come by.

It was only after Janet Ritter's death (not her real name, since we cannot violate her secret either) that members of her family and close friends discovered what a powerful factor the Prayer in Secret had been in her life.

Janet was married to a successful New York journalist. In her forties she became an alcoholic. The best professional care could not cure her. Her defeat and self-loathing took a curious form. Often her husband would come home to their Park Avenue apartment to find his wife unconscious on the floor of her closet. Obsessed by a feeling of guilt during her drinking, Janet would often decide to clean out her closet. She would work at it desperately until she passed out. In the end, the closet held the clue to Janet's release. From the little that Janet told us, we have been able to piece the story together . . . .

On a particular day, she lay across her bed fighting a desperate inner battle. Thanks to Alcoholics Anonymous, she had been dry for two months. That morning she had an overwhelming urge for just one drink. She well knew that once she had one, a hundred more would never be enough. "God help me," she cried. "I can't let my husband and children down again."

On the nightstand beside her was a Bible bound in white leather—little used. That day, however, she opened the Bible by chance to the Sermon on the Mount. Her eyes fell on the word *closet* . . . . Instantly her attention was arrested. Closet! Her closet had become a symbol to her, a hated symbol.

> But thou, when thou prayest, enter into thy closet, and when thou hast shut thy door, pray to thy Father which is in secret; and thy Father which seeth in secret shall reward thee openly.
>
> Matthew 6:6

Pray in the closet? Why? Janet had no idea why. But that closet drew her as a magnet. Once again she found herself huddling in among her belongings. Only this time, she was praying, praying for release from her bondage.

The open reward that Jesus promised was given to Janet Ritter. She overcame her temptation for alcohol. In addition, her personality took on such magnestism that, five years after her death, I have seen the faces of friends glow when they speak of her.

Many of the details of her story we shall never uncover. We do know that after that morning, Jesus' formula for power became Janet's guide. She found that giving part of herself or her possessions, in secret, formed the base for rejuvenating her life.

Here are two incidents that came out inadvertently. A private school in New York was instructed to select a worthy girl from a slum district. She would be sent to school, all expenses paid. She must never know her benefactor.

A New York bachelor friend, ill with bronchitis, had a tureen of delicious soup and a tray of delicacies delivered to his door each day. The messenger gave no name; there was no name on the tray. In this case, the bachelor guessed and finally made Janet admit it.

Undoubtedly there was a long series of kindnesses—large and small—all kept secret. The rewards were so open that Janet Ritter's influence for good will go on and on. In addition, to an amazing degree, her personality took on that indefinable feminine charm and magnetism for which every woman longs.

If you feel that your prayers are ineffective, as we all do at times, I suggest you explore the formula for prayer that Jesus bequeathed to us. The world desperately needs the concentrated power that comes from praying in secret.

Our Secret

Father, I begin to see that You have decreed the Law of Secrecy all through Your Creation. Seeds secreted in the warm earth are invisible to all eyes but Yours during the long days of germination. Baby chicks hidden in the eggs do not cackle or crow during the weeks of incubation beneath the patient mother hen. Our creation too requires the months of seclusion in the dark of the womb. So I see that prayer, the highest form of creation, must also for a time be hidden with You for Your work to be accomplished.

Lord, here is a request dear to my heart: ____________________ ________. It strengthens my faith to know that You want this petition to be our secret; that as I hide my request in You, I have touched the creative heart of the universe.

So I leave this prayer with You, Father. As day follows day with no results visible to me, give me the gift of knowing that since You care for me more tenderly than for any seeds or eggs, Your work of Creation on my behalf is going on just as surely. How I thank You! In the beauty and strength of Jesus' name I pray. *Amen.*

A suggestion: for most of us a bit of dramatization helps. You could write out your Prayer in Secret, date it, and insert it between the pages of a little-used Bible close to a promise that speaks to you, such as Matthew 6:3, 4. Then leave it there until your prayer is answered. C.M.

Marjorie Holmes

How Can I Find You, God?

Marjorie Holmes simply yet succinctly puts into prayer to the "living, loving, always listening God" those problems, emotions, and decisions—the everyday and the great—which every woman faces. Author of *I've Got to Talk to Somebody, God* and *Two From Galilee,* syndicated columnist, teacher of writing courses at several colleges, and lecturer are among the many hats she wears in addition to being Mrs. Lynn Mighell and the mother of four grown children.

No Limits On Love

Who are you, God? Where are you? How do I find you? How can I truly know you?

The heavens declare your glory, the whole world is witness to your wonders. I find you in nature, in birth and death and the very pain that is my lot. All beauty speaks to me of you, all the creative arts. And I can speak to you through prayer; your own Holy Spirit responds.

Yet one thing more I must have truly to be one with you. And that is love . . . . Yes, of course I love, or these things would not have meaning. But if I am to merge deeply with your being I must love more. Not just wind and water and stars and sky because they are of you; not merely my work or books and music and painting, not even my times of prayer. I must love my fellow human beings.

Oh, but I do, I do! I insist . . . . And your voice seems to ask: "How much? Enough to refrain from hurting? Enough to forgive? Enough to sacrifice, to serve, to rescue? Do you really love your neighbor as yourself?"

I can only whimper—I try, I'm trying. After all, I'm only human, and there are so many demands. There are limits on my energy, my time, my money, my strength. Limits on—my love!

And God seems to reply: "There are no limits on love."

No limits on his love—no. (For God is omnipotent, and God is love.) But how about mine? I am not God, far from it. I am a weak, faulty person. I get busy and angry, hold grudges sometimes; I blurt out words that hurt, words I regret. I do my best to help people but I can't help everyone—every neighbor who gets sick, needs a baby-sitter or a willing shoulder to cry on, every writer who presents me with a manuscript. (How would I take care of my own family, how would I get my own writing done?) Yet they tug at my heart, all these needs on my own doorstep . . . As for the needs of the world! I can't contribute to every cause, however worthy (so many it's hard even to know what the worthy ones *are*) . . . As for the world's poor—

The raggedy children in Israel, swarming around every tourist. Hands open for begging, or filled with cheap trinkets to sell—olivewood rosaries, strings of carved camels and donkeys. To give to one or buy from one is to be besieged. I had to flee from one little mob who had literally attacked. Scared? yes, but oddly not angry. Too hurt to be angry, hurt by their haunted faces, the anguish of the poverty that set them on "a rich American." Stricken at my utter helplessness before such need.

No limits on love . . . Is that what you mean, Lord? Even powerless and frightened I could still love those children. For you place no limits on love.

Thinking of that, I feel better. God, in his infinite understanding, knows our limitations. Of time, money, physical strength. He expects us to do what we can (and it's really quite a lot) but only what we can. He makes allowances for all that we fail to accomplish, so long as we love.

That is the secret, just to love . . . But when we *can* help, *do* help, then we are quick with his living presence. And there is no joy like it . . . .

Finding God through loving is not all joy, far from it. Pain is very much a part of it. It makes me vulnerable. I cannot ignore the cross of another; even if I am powerless to lift it, I stagger with the weight of it on my heart.

No, no, please! My own cross is heavy, there are lashes on my back, too, I've got wounds of my own to heal.

Give me the joy of helping, Lord, spare me the hurting. Especially when I can't help . . . Then I remember your words: "Blessed are the merciful."

And I know that without mercy, whatever its cost, I can't love either God or man.

Two by the Side of the Road

Mercy. Inseparable from love. At least in the eyes of God. I look in my concordance for the word *mercy* in all its forms. I look there for the word *love*. To my surprise they occupy equal space. The Bible speaks of mercy as often as it does of love!

Mercy. Compassion. Kindness. "Love suffereth long, and is kind."

Impossible then to love anyone or anything without this kindness. Cruelty has no place in love. If you love an animal you cannot be cruel to it (at least without awful remorse). Or intentionally cruel to the mate or child you love. I heard someone say: "He hurts the most the ones he loves the most." "On purpose?" "Sure, all the time. He enjoys it. But later he's usually sorry."

This isn't God's kind of love, it can't be. It's a distortion of love. A sado-masochistic self-love masquerading. Genuine love wants to relive pain, not inflict it. And when the demons in us take over (as they often do), when we say or do cruel things to those we love, then our own suffering later may surpass theirs . . . . This remorse, this awful devastation—isn't it the stern side of God showing us that cruelty has no place in love?

Only mercy. Compassion. Understanding . . . To identify. Empathize. To know how hurting *feels* . . . Do unto others as ye would have them do unto you.

And this identification extends beyond those close to you. It includes that poor kid scribbling his poems on grubby envelopes in prison, and even the *picture* of an abandoned child . . . . It makes you one with every individual whose need you see. A swift and poignant merging so that you *are* that person for an instant. Even that insecure stranger at the party, nervously hoping someone will speak to him. Because you know how it feels (and can't stand how it feels) you go to him, hand outstretched . . . . You *are* that suffering patient on a stretcher, or the distraught man or woman standing by. And the hurt is too much, you've got to do something to assuage it, if only by an encouraging word.

Jesus, dear Jesus, I sometimes envy you! When you felt pity for people you had only to reach out and touch them and they were healed. You could make them walk again, you could restore their sight . . . . I feel such pity for people, but so helpless before their plight. Jesus, dear Jesus, show me what to do.

The Good Samaritan. That parable was for all of us. That parable was for me . . . . Oh, but it takes courage to be a Good Samaritan, it can look silly, even be dangerous. It's not safe to go to anybody's rescue any more, not even by daylight on a busy street. New York, especially. People don't pay any attention, just walk on by.

And I'm in New York now, taking a walk before a luncheon appointment, on a bitterly cold day. And across the street, in front of a funeral home, lies a body. Heavens, don't they even pick up their *bodies?* Don't look, none of your business, hurry on by . . . . But what if—? Never mind, look in store windows, beautiful clothes, forget that—*but what if it isn't a body?* None of your business, don't be a hick . . . . Okay, okay, cross the street, walk back just to be sure, it's probably gone by now . . . . Only it isn't, and people are stepping around it, paying no attention, although you see it moving, hear its feeble cries—"Help me . . . somebody!" Okay, *okay,* hick, chicken out-of-towner, break down, make a fool of yourself, ask what's the matter?

He's shaking, haggard, sick. He needs food, something warm in his stomach. If you give him some money will he please go in out of the cold and eat? (You are begging for yourself!) He agress, sobbing, and you hand him a dollar, escape. (Fool, he'll use it for drink.) When you look back he waves so plaintively you can't stand it. So *go* back, *go* back, idiot. "Your problem is alcohol, isn't it? Will you go to A.A. if I can get you there? They'll help you."

"Lady . . . I'll go . . . anywhere!"

Try to find a phone booth, try to find their number. They say they can't come after him, but if I can bring him by taxi . . . Try to get a taxi . . . . He is sitting up now, and another woman has stopped to talk to him. "Would you like for me to go with you?" she asks. Thank God. Especially since the headquarters prove to be in an undesirable section. (Could you have gotten him safely up those stairs by yourself, hick? Would the cab driver, sweet guy that he seemed to be, have helped you?) No matter, the other Good Samaritan supports his other side . . . . And they welcome him kindly, assure us he will have medical attention, food, a bed.

Leaving, the woman and I agree we, too, will sleep better tonight, knowing that. And that we could use some coffee ourselves. "He was worth saving," she says. "He's an educated man—did you notice his diction? And his manners, even so sick. When he said he'd never forget us he meant it. He's a good but very sick man."

Belatedly, we exchange names—and gasp. She is Ann Williams-Heller, well-known nutritionist. She writes for the same magazines I do, knows the same people! We fall into each other's arms, friends . . . . She came to this country as an Austrian war refugee. Now, years later, love brought us together. Out of all the people swarming the New York streets, the same life line from the same God drew us together at the side of someone who was suffering.

". . . whatsoever good thing any man doeth, the same shall he receive of the Lord . . . ."

It's not always that swift, that clear. Now I must record the incident of the old woman in Haifa, not to exalt myself, heaven knows, but only to try to understand the peculiar anguish of another love shared . . . .

She was bent over, heavy and stooped, with a homemade crutch under one arm, and in the other hand a knobby stick on which to lean. At her feet, a string bag filled with groceries. Evidently she had been shopping and discovered she could not carry them. She was weeping and making pitiful gestures to people thrusting past on the steep hot street.

I halted, torn. Our bus was making only a brief stop. Long enough to explore some of the art shops. I was rushing up the hill to look at some mosaics glimpsed in a window. But my heart would not let me pass. I halted, picked up the heavy bag, and tried to walk with her a little way.

Then I saw that her poor old feet in their run-over shoes could scarcely make it. She had to pause every few inches and point to one of them, so swollen it had broken through the thin flopping slipper. I set down the bag and knelt to examine it; the shoe was so broken and dusty it had rubbed the flesh raw. How to help, what to do? I tried putting a Kleenex in the sole to ease it a little bit. I caressed her foot with my fingers. Then I stood up and said, "Lean on me." And thus we progressed a little way.

Meanwhile, I was trying to enlist the aid of an Israeli soldier—anyone who might know where she lived and come to her aid. But if they understood they gave no sign; they simply shrugged and went on. All I could do was talk to her encouragingly in a language she did not understand. And when she had to stop again the hurt was too much for both of us, the love; I embraced her and kissed her and we clung together, so at least she realized that somebody cared. And she gazed at me through her tragic old eyes beneath the ragged shawl, and the tears flowed afresh.

The others were returning to the bus, calling, "Come on!" I would have to leave her. In desperation I hailed a boy of about fifteen and pleaded, "Do you speak English? Do you know where this woman lives? Can't you please carry her things home?" To my relief, he nodded, took up the bag, and set off down the hill. Behind him she continued to plod, inching along, halted again and again by the agonies of age. The last I saw was that stooped figure still making its tortuous way downhill in the blazing sun.

And my heart cried out after her. I felt as if I was abandoning her, as if I ought to give up all the comforts and joys of my own life to make her life easier . . . in that awful moment of recognition she was my mother! She was all the mothers who have borne children and grown old and crippled and live in poverty and torment as they struggle through their final days. I wanted to help her. I wanted to know that she lay on clean sheets in a cool house with somebody nearby to soothe her and keep her company.

I wanted to heal her. And to be able to do so little hurt so much.

I said that I sometimes envy Jesus. Now I realize . . . he couldn't heal everyone either, he couldn't provide for all the poor. There were simply too many. He, too, was limited by time and energy. And if *he* had limitations, how much greater are my human limitations. And if I suffer because of them, how much more he must have suffered for those people he had to turn away. (And must suffer still for us.)

But this I must remember. There were and are no limits on his love. All he asks of me is that I put no limits on my love.

Grant Me the Kind of Love

that does not keep old scores.
    Let me be unfettered
    from old tallies
    from old whiplashes
    from old borrowing and not returning.
Let me forget all these.
The straw-stuffed scarecrow
kind of love with coat and hat
retrieved from old trunks—
let me own none of these.
    Let me know every morning-new day
    kind of love: dew-wet, garden-fresh,
    growing kind of love
a not-afraid-of-being-hurt,
or wounded kind of love—
a love that does not syncopate,
or change the meaning of the word.
A love that does not shun toll roads—
nor yet mind byroads
    and never counts the cost.

WILMA BURTON